Super
Natural

Super Natural

Tobie Puttock

With contributions by
Georgia Puttock

Photography by
Julie Renouf

LANTERN

an imprint of
PENGUIN BOOKS

Contents

Foreword 1

Introduction 3

The vegan pantry 6

Meal preparation and planning 11

Banana, walnut and chia bread 14

Chocolate, cinnamon
and apricot breakfast bars 17

Chia, coconut
and berry parfaits 18

Apple and cinnamon
breakfast cookies 20

Chocolate chia seed puddings 21

Banana, pecan, chia
and strawberry pancakes 23

Green smoothie formula 24

Scrambled chickpeas 26

Breakfast burritos 27

Potato rosti 30

Roast mushrooms with
thyme and garlic breadcrumbs 31

Homemade baked beans 34

Pumpkin, ginger and
coriander soup, hemp seeds
and cashew cream 38

Broccoli and kale soup 41

Minestrone, risoni
and kale pesto 42

Lentil, spinach and sage soup 44

Pumpkin and sweet potato
soup with sambal 45

Parsnip and leek soup with
black pepper breadcrumbs 46

Pea and mint falafel flatbreads 48

Fresh tomato pizza with
kale pesto and olives 52

Eggplant parmigiana 54

Fried tofu sandwich with
Japanese barbecue sauce 56

Sweet potato chips
with chilli and dill 59

Fig, hazelnut
and thyme pizza 60

Cucumber, hummus
and flatbread 62

Kale, lemon, garlic
and seed salad 65

Shaved asparagus, pear,
walnut and rocket salad 66

Roast pumpkin, freekeh,
lime and coriander salad 69

Classic coleslaw 70

Cucumber, sesame
and chilli salad 71

Avocado, sprout
and cucumber salad 73

Carrot, chickpea,
cumin and mint salad 74

Lentil, mushroom
and asparagus salad 76

Tomato and beetroot salad 78

Celeriac, radicchio
and fennel salad 81

Witlof, apple, radish
and walnut salad 82

Zucchini carpaccio with
pine nuts, sultanas and lemon 84

Grilled cos with
chilli and almonds 87

Shaved fennel, melon
and green olive salad 88

Potato, horseradish
and tarragon salad 90

Spicy chilli beans 94

Penne with roasted tomato,
garlic and olives 96

Orecchiette with
cauliflower and peppery
breadcrumbs 99

Spaghetti with mushrooms,
thyme and garlic 100

Zucchini spaghetti, peas,
asparagus and kale pesto 102

Stuffed butternut pumpkin
with sage, chestnuts
and cranberries 105

Whole roast cauliflower,
romesco and avocado 106

Black bean burger, sriracha,
cucumber, coriander and cos 108

Lentil, sweet potato
and mushroom shepherd's pie 110

Braised green beans with
cherry tomatoes and paprika 114

Risi e bisi 115

Whole roast celeriac with
thyme, garlic and
black olive sauce 116

Over-roasted beetroot with
walnut and horseradish cream 119

Slow-grilled cauliflower steaks
with miso, soy, maple
and sesame seeds 120

Mushroom and
chestnut wellington 122

Barbecued asparagus with
harissa breadcrumbs 126

Barbecued corn with
sriracha aioli 129

Braised eggplant, tomatoes,
capers and basil 130

Braised zucchini with
cherry tomatoes and mint 131

Slow-braised fennel,
garlic, capers and lemon 132

Hasselback sweet potatoes 134

Crispy brussels sprouts,
parsley and sambal 136

Kale, garlic, shallots,
capers and lemon 138

Sesame and maple carrots
with baba ghanoush 141

Roast capsicum,
capers, olives, chilli 142

Charred leeks with romesco 145

Cold spinach with
toasted sesame seeds 146

Mashed potato with
lemon and olive oil 147

Shoestring chips with
rosemary and sea salt 149

Sticky eggplant with
miso and sesame 150

Chocolate, date
and walnut brownies 154

Banana fritters with
cinnamon and nutmeg 156

Rhubarb and coconut crumble 158

Apple strudel 160

Grilled peaches, vanilla,
maple and nuts 164

Banana and berry ice-cream 167

Chocolate mousse with
berries and pistachios 168

Banoffee pie pots 170

Chocolate and
salted caramel tart 172

Summer pudding 174

Saffron and cardamom
poached pears with
cashew cream 178

Roasted pineapple with
chilli, mint and maple 180

Pumpkin and olive oil
spice cake 182

Rice pudding
and strawberry jam 186

Black olive sauce 190

Romesco sauce 192

Tomato basil sauce 194

Chimichurri 195

Harissa 197

Sambal 198

Chickpea hummus 200

Edamame hummus 201

Kale and cashew pesto 202

Baba ghanoush 204

Homemade breadcrumbs 205

Italian flatbread 206

Basic pizza dough 207

Sweet pastry 208

Caramel sauce 209

Nut butter 210

Nut and seed mix 213

Further reading 214

Acknowledgements 217

Index 218

Foreword

What a total pleasure it is to be writing the foreword for my dear old friend Tobie's cracking new cookbook. Tobie and I met over 20 years ago when we were both starting out as young chefs at London's iconic River Café, under the expert guidance of legends Ruth Rogers and the late Rose Gray.

Like me, Tobie arrived at The River Café with a passion for all things Italy, and I remember he'd just come back from a formative time living and cooking in the Italian mountains. He was also with me during that incredible time when *The Naked Chef* really took off, and life super-charged up a level!

Tobie helped me open my beautiful London restaurant Fifteen as head chef, and later went on to open Melbourne's Fifteen back in his homeland, Australia. Since those early days, Tobie has gone on to even more great and fun things, writing several fantastic cookbooks, creating food lines, and developing distinctive techniques and recipe styles.

As he explains in the introduction, this book is part of Tobie's evolution as a chef – these new vegan recipes are tapping into a whole new way of thinking about plant-based food, which is increasingly popular across the planet. For me, this is perfect timing. I think it's important to say that this book isn't just for vegans and vegetarians – it's almost more for the meat eaters who so desperately need inspiration on the veg front. Eating more veg is definitely not only good for your health, it also helps you ramp up the deliciousness! When you follow Tobie's simple, brilliant recipes, you'll see this is a real celebration. I'm a meat eater myself, but having a few legitimate veggie meals each week frees up a bit of cash, and that should mean you can afford to trade up to the best, higher-welfare meat when you do eat it. And of course, choosing organic dairy is an easy swap. Having this balance allows you to be more dynamic with your food budget. Whatever your food journey or choices, I believe in pushing a more plant-based diet, and at the same time supporting better farming practices across the board.

When it comes to cooking, the thing that's always struck me about Tobie is his passion and enthusiasm – and you get that by the bucketload in this book. His slow-braised fennel and capers dish (see page 132) takes me straight back to our River Café days, and I can't wait to make the orecchiette with cauliflower and peppery breadcrumbs (see page 99). For me, all the beautiful pastas, soups and salads in this book are the best of seasonal cooking. And don't even get me started on those beautiful puds! It's an amazing collection of comforting, colourful, vegan recipes – with real heart and soul. Well done, Tobie – smashed it, mate!

Jamie Oliver

Introduction

There's a story behind this book. You see, I've been cooking for more than half my life, and I've worked hard and been lucky enough to have now written and published this, my fifth cookbook. Each book has been a little more 'me' than the last as I've grown as a chef and as a man, and this book you hold in your hands is the most important to me so far.

In 2018, we've reached an age where information about our food is more readily available. Practices once hidden from view are being exposed to the public despite governments' attempted ag-gags, and scientists worldwide are proving on a daily basis the enormous cost that our regular eating habits and behaviours are having to our health, our environment and the other beings on our planet. The way we eat now is also terrible for our future food security, and is increasingly being exposed as morally corrupt.

The flipside to this is that with the constant inundation of information – documentaries about where our food comes from, a new fad diet every week, conflicting information all over the place – it can all be too much to process. In my experience people want to do the right thing, but change is hard: the wrong things are cheaper than the right things, we're confused and, when it comes to the crunch, we don't know who to trust. Reverting to what we've always done is just easiest.

Last year my wife, Georgia, (who became a fish-eating vegetarian over a decade ago when confronted with *The River Cottage Meat Book* by Hugh Fearnley-Whittingstall) sat me down to watch some documentaries on food production. As a chef, I had an idea of what I thought was going on, but to actually allow myself to see the realities of intensive food production was shocking. I've worked with meat for so long that I thought I'd come to terms with death. I knew roughly how an animal was slaughtered and I've butchered many a carcass during my years as a chef. I knew a bit about the egg industry too, but it was milk production that really got to me. I've been drinking milk my whole life, and of course I know where it comes from – but for some reason I hadn't really questioned it any further than that.

When I started researching the process for myself, it horrified me more than I ever could have imagined. I discovered that, after being artificially impregnated against her will, a cow is pregnant for 283 days (similar to humans), gives birth, and then is immediately separated from her calf so that none of her precious milk is wasted. The image of the mother moving desperately towards her calf as a gate is closed in between them was enough to make me really rethink my relationship to milk.

Whether you think you can come to terms with this or not, I suspect you know in your heart that it isn't right. We know that animals are sentient beings, that they feel pain just like we do. Imagine that was your baby taken away from you and then you were hooked up to a machine and milked until you ran dry, only to have the whole process repeated again and again, until the end.

The reason ag-gag laws exist is to shield people from witnessing these despicable practices – not for your own good because they're distressing, but for financial reasons. This is the most awful part: it's all just about money. It's not about survival for us – our bodies don't need cow's milk to grow into healthy humans, cows are a completely different species. It's just become culturally normal for us to drink milk, the same way that eating dog meat is standard practice in some Asian countries.

Luckily, now, the tide is shifting. We are at a precipice and we are wising up to what we need to do to make lasting change. Silicon Valley investors are rushing to fund vegan start-ups and, incredibly, Bill Gates's Beyond Meat plant-based burgers are being sold in the meat section of Whole Foods and Safeway in the US. Richard Branson's into it too. From the other end of the spectrum, there are an increasing number of small producers within the agriculture industry who are trying to change the standards of animal production to regulate for the most humane methods possible. Some of these people are my friends and colleagues here in Australia, and when I see their passion I'm so glad because without them, change won't happen – it's a slow process, and I know a lot of people will continue to eat meat and animal products for years to come. But facing up to where your food really comes from is key.

So back to me. As I write these words I'm 43 years old. Our pantry at home is 90 per cent vegan, I enjoy a cheese toastie from time to time, I eat fish every week or so and on rare occasions I enjoy a small piece of steak or a slice of porchetta if it's on offer. Becoming 'reducetarian' wasn't an overnight decision but a result of gathering information and experience. Since Georgia has been pescatarian for more than ten years, we're used to not eating red meat, pork or chicken at home, which probably made it easier. We try out different ingredients, make the most of fresh produce and have fun creating new meat-free meals. We get all the nutrients we need from the various plant-based recipes I cook or use a supplement if need be – and we feel great!

As you will discover from cooking these recipes, they are satisfying and delicious. Not once during the creation of this book did I have the feeling that a recipe was missing something, or I was going without – everything is complete.

I very much hope that this book gives you the tools to add some plant power into your diet. Becoming a full vegan is no mean feat, but imagine how much difference it would make if *everyone* ate just a bit less meat and dairy?

Once last thing: if you don't already know much about the food industry, take some time to understand how your food made it to the plate. Knowledge is power.

P.S. A note from Georgia

I'm so proud to have played a part in the evolution of this book. To have even a small role in creating solutions to the world's problems is a privilege, and that is truly what Tobie and I intend with *SuperNatural*. We're not asking anyone to become hard-line vegans (I tried it myself ten years ago and found it incredibly hard, though fortunately it's much easier nowadays). But if these recipes make animal-free cooking delicious and enjoyable to you, then you get to be part of the solution too.

The human brain has an incredible knack for filtering out that which we do not want to see or hear, but if we learn more about food and where it comes from and listen less to marketing and cultural norms, we have the power to make lasting change. For further reading, Brian Kateman's *The Reducetarian Solution* is absolutely brilliant and makes a great case for becoming a 'reducetarian': someone who makes an effort to reduce their animal consumption at their own pace, instead of pitting meat-heads against vegan sterotypes.

During the process of reducing our intake of animal products, I embarked on a nutritional fact-finding mission to ensure Tobie, our daughter Birdie and I would be consuming the right balance of essential macro and micronutrients. The information I obtained from speaking to nutritionists and reading textbooks and scientific journals was so interesting that I became completely engrossed with the subject matter, and I still am to this day.

As I learned about the nutritional benefits of the plants we eat, my enthusiasm for eating a larger variety of plant foods skyrocketed – so I've shared some of my research throughout this book in the form of 'vegan bites' at the end of some of the recipes.

Finally, a note on nutrition: government recommended daily intakes or RDIs tend to be quite broad to encompass different people at different life stages. Please see a certified nutritionist if you have any questions about your personal nutritional needs.

The vegan pantry

For the past 20 years, my pantry probably looked typical of an Italian chef's: various olive oils, vinegars, a couple of different spices and lots of herbs, grains and so on. I was in the land of garlic, basil and tomatoes for so long! But after some time out of the professional kitchen I've befriended a lot of spices I hadn't really used before – simply because I hadn't been taught how to use them – plus different chillies, flours and so on. It makes me realise that vegan cooking has definitely made me a better cook – I've learnt to understand how ingredients work on a deeper level, and you can too.

Spices

Spices are everything in vegetarian and vegan cooking – they are your best friend and you need to get to know them. They will allow you to make simple dishes with just a few ingredients that are incredibly layered and complex in flavour.

cardamom	cinnamon sticks	cumin seeds	paprika
cayenne pepper	cloves	fennel seeds	sesame seeds
chilli flakes	coriander seeds	garam masala	turmeric
ground cinnamon	ground cumin	whole nutmeg	

Herbs

Herbs have always been an important part of my cooking and in this book, they definitely bring dishes to life. Fresh herbs are always my first choice but can lead to wastage. In order to reduce that, dry out leftover fresh herbs by laying them out on a baking tray lined with baking paper and sitting them in a warm part of the kitchen until dried and crisp. You can then keep them in zip-lock bags or crush them and store them in jars to be used through the bases of sauces for added flavour.

basil	dill	curly-leaf parsley	tarragon
coriander	mint	flat-leaf parsley	

Legumes, grains, nuts, seeds

You can of course use dried beans of all varieties but, to be honest, I almost always use canned at home. Some dried beans need to be soaked overnight whereas canned are ready to rock in seconds. Some grains, like freekeh, don't take too long to cook and they can also last in an airtight container in the fridge for a few days.

black beans
cannellini beans
fava beans
pinto beans
red kidney
  beans
soybeans
chickpeas

peas
couscous
freekeh
lentils
quinoa
rice
chia seeds
hemp seeds

linseeds (flax
  seeds)
pepitas (pumpkin
  seeds)
poppy seeds
sunflower seeds
almonds
cashews

chestnuts
hazelnuts
macadamias
pecans
pine nuts
pistachios
walnuts

Other

My cooking is always evolving and my pantry reflects this.

olive oil
extra virgin olive
  oil
avocado oil
sesame oil
coconut oil
shredded coconut
fine polenta
semolina

almond meal
plain flour
self-raising flour
wholemeal flour
cornflour (corn
  starch)
baking powder
bicarbonate of
  soda

brown rice
  malt syrup
pure maple syrup
icing sugar
dried apricots
cranberries
soy sauce
sriracha chilli
  sauce

tamari sauce
balsamic vinegar
red wine vinegar
rice wine vinegar

Meal preparation and planning

I've structured this book a little differently from my previous books, which had obvious dinner or breakfast recipes – this one starts in the morning and progresses through the day to finish in the evening. So while there are some recipes like pancakes that are traditionally eaten first thing, others – a soup, a salad or a cauliflower steak – can be eaten at various times of the day without needing to be defined as a particular meal. I've given you a guide to when I think the dishes are best eaten simply by their placement in the book, but *SuperNatural* belongs to you now – so dirty up the pages and cook from it as you please.

In each recipe, look out for the symbols letting you know if the dish can be supersized ((↑)), meaning that you can easily double, triple or quadruple the size of the recipe to make a big quantity that will last you a few days (or if you're cooking for a crowd). There's also a symbol ((✳)) to let you know if the dish freezes well so then you can get into the good stuff, batch cooking and freezing, which will make life much easier.

Generally, salads don't scale up so well – but some of the grain salads do, and if this is the case I would recommend leaving out any leafy parts and the dressing until you are ready to eat. Get into the habit of popping the dressing in a little container, the herbs in another and then bring it together at the last moment.

I've also included a time key ((🕑)) in the recipes so you can work out at a glance if you'll have enough time to make something – they're categorised as quick (less than 30 minutes), medium (30–60 minutes) or slow (1 hour or longer). Try to put aside a few hours a week to batch cook and plan your week. I use a meal planner to work out most meals in advance for the week. That way I can shop, cook and be prepared for what the week throws at me. It's great feeling organised, and I tend not to make bad food choices when I know I've got delicious stuff waiting for me at home.

(All recipes in this book have been developed using a fan-forced oven. If using a conventional oven, you'll generally need to increase the oven temperature by 20°C, but please note that cooking times may vary depending on your individual oven.)

Banana, walnut and chia bread

This bread is a winner and works so nicely with a spreading of my homemade nut butter (see page 210). I personally like this slightly toasted and it freezes beautifully so go ahead and make a few loaves and freeze them up. Taking some time to cook before the week starts can be really enjoyable and will get you feeling all prepared, so if you can, carve out a few hours on a Sunday afternoon and pick three recipes that are suitable for supersizing to cook, portion and freeze. I do this all the time and it really means that I'm actually only cooking a few nights a week and on the others it's just a case of pulling pre-prepared recipes out of the freezer, eating and relaxing. Too easy!

⏱
Slow

extra virgin olive oil or coconut oil, for greasing	¼ teaspoon ground nutmeg
4 super ripe bananas (about 450 g), roughly chopped	sea salt
	1½ cups (225 g) plain flour
½ cup (110 g) firmly packed brown sugar	1½ teaspoons baking powder
½ cup (125 ml) extra virgin olive oil or coconut oil	½ teaspoon bicarbonate of soda
1 teaspoon vanilla essence	1 tablespoon chia seeds
½ teaspoon ground cinnamon	½ cup (50 g) walnuts, lightly crushed

GF
If substituting regular flour with gluten-free flour

Preheat the oven to 180°C. Grease a 23 cm × 17 cm loaf tin using a little olive oil or coconut oil, then line with baking paper and lightly grease the paper.

Put the bananas and sugar in a mixing bowl and mash well with a fork. Fold through the olive oil or coconut oil, vanilla, cinnamon, nutmeg and a pinch of salt.

Sift the flour, baking powder and bicarbonate of soda together in a medium bowl. Using a wooden spoon, fold the flour mixture through the banana mixture. Fold through the chia seeds and walnuts.

Spoon the mixture into the prepared tin and smooth the surface with the back of a spoon. Bake for 35–40 minutes or until a skewer inserted into the centre of the loaf comes out clean. Transfer to a wire rack and leave until almost completely cool before removing from tin.

TIP: The bread will keep for up to 3 days in an airtight container, or can be wrapped in plastic film and frozen for up to 2 weeks.

CHIA SEEDS

Now considered a 'nutraceutical product', chia seeds have a ridiculously extensive list of nutritional properties, including: very high levels of polyunsaturated fatty acids (omega-3s – hard to otherwise obtain in plant-based diets), B vitamins, calcium, phosphorus and potassium, polyphenolic compounds and antioxidants, and high levels of protein compared to similar cereals. There are over 30 grams of dietary fibre per 100 grams of chia, which is equal to a whopping 100 per cent of the recommended daily intake (RDI) of dietary fibre – and fibre has been shown to be associated with a reduced risk of type 2 diabetes, heart disease and some cancers.

Tobie
Puttock

Chocolate, cinnamon and apricot breakfast bars

I am not sure why but, for me personally, sitting around relaxing over a bowl of granola while reading the paper is something I never seem to have the luxury to do. When I started cooking I was in the kitchen at 6am. I also seem to be my most productive in the early hours so generally I hop out of bed and get on with it, then before I know it, it's 11am and I'm hangry. So, let me introduce you to my breakfast bar. It's essentially a muesli bar like we have all had but this one is without added sugars. You can customise it as well by swapping out the almonds for another nut or a combo of nuts and seeds – and of course the dried apricots can be swapped out for other dried fruits like cherries.

Quick +
setting time

2 cups (180 g) rolled oats

½ cup (50 g) quinoa flakes

½ cup (80 g) chia seeds

½ cup (70 g) slivered almonds

½ cup (75 g) dried apricot halves, roughly chopped

½ cup (85 g) dark vegan chocolate, roughly chopped

¾ cup (210 g) nut butter (see page 210)

⅓ cup (80 ml) pure maple syrup or brown rice malt syrup

2 tablespoons coconut oil

good pinch of cinnamon

1 cup (170 g) seeded prunes

Line a large baking tray with baking paper.

Put rolled oats, quinoa, chia seeds, slivered almonds, dried apricots and the chocolate in a large bowl and stir until well combined.

Put the nut butter, maple syrup, coconut oil and cinnamon in a small saucepan over low heat. Cook, stirring, until melted and smooth.

Put the prunes in a food processor and process until a smooth puree. Fold prune puree through the nut butter mixture. Pour nut butter mixture over the oat mixture and mix with a wooden spoon until well combined.

Using clean hands, shape mixture (about ⅓ cup mixture per bar) into rectangles, approximately 10 cm × 2 cm. Pop them onto the prepared tray, then place in fridge for at least 1–2 hours or until set.

OATS

Why love these breakfast bars? Firstly, the fibre: increased fibre consumption has been linked to the enrichment of gut microbiota, an increasingly important area of study with major implications for overall good health. Secondly, oats have a low glycemic index (GI), are high in protein for a cereal, and contain lots of vitamins and minerals and support the body's immune system. Make sure to buy the whole rolled oat variety, not the quick-cook, flavoured options.

Chia, coconut and berry parfaits

In my previous life as a hardened chef I bundled chia seeds up with daisy chains, hip hop yoga and people that say 'beautiful soul' a lot – but let's cut through the hype. This little seed can swell up to nine times its size with moisture, making it an incredible ingredient for creating all sorts of dishes from smoothies to puddings. And as chia seeds have very little flavour themselves, they will take on the flavour of whatever liquid they absorb – nifty.

Quick +
setting time

½ cup (80 g) chia seeds

2 cups (500 ml) unsweetened almond milk or soy milk

¼ cup (60 ml) pure maple syrup

1 tablespoon vanilla extract

2 cups (220 g) granola

3 cups (450 g) fresh or frozen mixed berries, thawed if using frozen

1 tablespoon shredded coconut (optional)

Put the chia, milk, maple syrup and vanilla in a large bowl and stir to combine. Cover with plastic film and place in fridge overnight.

Put a layer of chia mixture, granola and berries in 4 individual serving bowls, glasses or jars. Repeat so you have 2 layers of each, finishing with some shredded coconut (if using).

GF

Tobie Puttock

Apple and cinnamon breakfast cookies

I love this type of cooking so much. Normally cookies need a binder like eggs and flour but in this recipe, I use the apple to do the binding and of course bring flavour to the cookie itself, and you can make these cookies in no time at all. The apple can also be replaced with banana or pear – or live on the edge and do a bit of both.

Quick

2 cups (180 g) rolled oats	good pinch of cinnamon
2 apples, cored, coarsely grated	1 tablespoon pure maple syrup

Preheat oven to 180°C. Line a large baking tray with baking paper.

Put the oats, apple, cinnamon and maple syrup in a large mixing bowl. Using clean hands mix until well combined. Form the mixture into 12 evenly sized balls, really pressing the mixture together.

Pop the balls onto the prepared tray and flatten with the palm of your hand. Make sure there is about 5 cm between each cookie.

Bake for 15 minutes or until golden. Transfer to a wire rack, then set aside to cool completely.

TIP: Cookies will store in an airtight container for up to 1 week.

CINNAMON

Delicious-tasting, comfortingly fragrant and so much more, in laboratory studies, cinnamon may have antimicrobial and anti-inflammatory effects, and there is evidence it may help reduce blood sugar and LDL cholesterol.

Chocolate chia seed puddings

Serves 4

These are genius, and they are insanely easy to make. For sure you need to get a little prepared and muster the energy a few hours or the night before to mix together some chia seeds, milk and a couple of other bits and pieces – which will take a total of 2 minutes. But this means breakfast is done! You can even do these puddings in little jars. They will keep for a couple of days so you can make 2 days' worth, top with berries at the last minute and skip off to work. Have a lovely day!

Quick +
setting time

350 ml unsweetened almond milk

60 g chia seeds

2½ tablespoons cacao or unsweetened cocoa powder

2½ tablespoons pure maple syrup

good pinch of ground cinnamon

pinch of sea salt

fresh berries (strawberries, blueberries, raspberries), to serve

Put all the ingredients into a food processor and process until smooth.

Transfer to an airtight container or 4 individual jars and cover. Place in fridge overnight, or for at least 3–5 hours, until it forms a pudding-like consistency. Serve topped with fresh berries.

GF

Banana, pecan, chia and strawberry pancakes

These pancakes are a favourite in my house. I make them all the time for my daughter, Birdie, and it's great to be able to watch her eating them with the peace of mind of knowing that she's getting a good serving of fruit to start the day. Like most of my recipes, this can be used as a starting point to play around with: try swapping out strawberries for other berries, and adding a dash of vanilla or a pinch of other spices such as ground nutmeg and cardamom.

Quick

1 cup (90 g) rolled oats	2 tablespoons chia seeds
1 cup (250 ml) soy milk	1 super ripe banana, roughly chopped
pinch of sea salt	1 tablespoon extra virgin olive oil
pinch of cinnamon	1 cup (200 g) strawberries, halved
⅓ cup (50 g) plain or wholemeal flour	1 tablespoon pecans, lightly crushed
2 teaspoons baking powder	1 tablespoon pure maple syrup

Pop the oats, soy milk, salt, cinnamon, flour, baking powder, chia seeds and banana into a food processor and process until smooth.

Drizzle olive oil into a large non-stick frying pan and heat over medium–low heat. Use a scrunched-up piece of paper towel to evenly rub the oil over the base of the pan.

Using ¼ cup (60 ml) mixture per pancake, cook 2–3 pancakes (allowing room for pancakes to spread) for 2 minutes or until bubbles appear on surface. Flip and cook for a further 2 minutes or until cooked through. Repeat to make 8 pancakes.

Serve pancakes topped with the strawberries, sprinkled with pecans and drizzled with maple syrup.

Green smoothie formula

We live about an hour out of Melbourne and I often drive in for meetings. On those days this is perfect to sip, while Led Zeppelin plays as we head along the highway – plus it keeps me going till lunch. If you're a bit smarty you can get yourself some plastic containers and pre-cut fruit for the next few days so you're ready to rock.

Quick

2 CUPS	+	2 CUPS	+	3 CUPS
leafy greens		liquid		ripe fruit
spinach		water		banana
kale		coconut water		mango
silver beet (Swiss chard)		almond milk		berries
				orange
				avocado
				peach
				apple
				pineapple

GF

Put leafy greens and liquid in a blender and blend until well combined. Add the fruit and blend again until thick and smooth.

Serve either in a tall glass or plastic flask to go.

POLYPHENOLS

Here's a tip that's especially important for vegetarians and vegans, relating to what you drink with your breakfast. Traditionally we tend to eat our breakfast alongside a cup of tea or coffee, drinks containing polyphenols – awesome antioxidants that benefit human health in a multitude of ways. However, studies have found that consuming black, green or herbal teas, coffee or cocoa during meals can reduce the absorption of non-haem iron (iron from plant-based sources) by as much as 85–90 per cent. So, to allow your body to absorb the iron present in your meal, wait an hour after eating before drinking your tea or coffee.

Tobie Puttock

Scrambled chickpeas

I'm not going to pretend to you that these are anything like scrambled eggs – they are not. I've never really liked eating eggs and so for me these are AMAZING. They are super quick to make and you can adjust the consistency with the aquafaba from the chickpeas (that's the liquid from the can) to make the scramble runnier or denser – and on that note, be sure to keep any leftover aquafaba if you are not using it so you can make my chocolate mousse (see page 168).

Quick

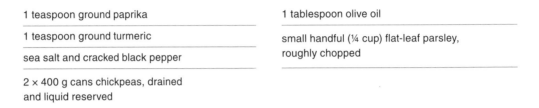

1 teaspoon ground paprika

1 teaspoon ground turmeric

sea salt and cracked black pepper

2 × 400 g cans chickpeas, drained
and liquid reserved

1 tablespoon olive oil

small handful (¼ cup) flat-leaf parsley,
roughly chopped

GF

Put the paprika, turmeric and a pinch of salt and pepper in a large bowl. Add enough of the reserved chickpea liquid to make a loose paste.

Add the chickpeas and roughly mash with a fork, making sure you distribute the spices evenly. Fold through about ½ cup (125 ml) of the reserved chickpea liquid to make the mixture nice and moist, add more if you wish.

Heat the olive oil in a large non-stick frying pan over medium heat. Add the chickpea mixture and cook, stirring often, until golden in colour, about 5–6 minutes. Fold through the parsley and serve.

TURMERIC

Turmeric is a brilliant and versatile spice that's long been used in Indian cooking and Ayurvedic medicine for its antioxidant and anti-inflammatory properties. A recent study found the potential health benefits of curcumin, the active ingredient in turmeric, can be significantly enhanced when it is ingested with black pepper: piperine, found in black pepper, aids the absorption of curcumin. That's why it's great to combine the two in recipes such as this one, and to add a sprinkle of black pepper to your turmeric lattes!

Tobie
Puttock

Breakfast burritos

I'm about to make a big call. This could be my favourite breakfast EVER. I had breakfast at a place in Encinitas, California, many moons ago and it was kind of like this: super refreshing with heat and acidity, a whisper of 'aren't I amazing' without the need for a lie down after.

1 small clove garlic

½ red onion

1 large tomato, diced

½ fresh green jalapeño chilli, finely chopped

sea salt and cracked black pepper

2 teaspoons extra virgin olive oil

4 large corn or flour vegan tortillas

½ × quantity scrambled chickpeas, warmed (see opposite)

1 large avocado, halved and sliced

large handful (1 cup) coriander sprigs

2 limes, halved

Medium

Finely grate the garlic and onion into a medium bowl. Add the tomato, jalapeño, a good pinch of salt and pepper and the olive oil. Stir until well combined and set aside.

Warm the tortillas as per packet instructions and lay them out side by side on a clean work surface.

Pop a quarter of the scrambled chickpeas on one quarter of each tortilla. Top with a couple of slices of avocado, followed by a spoonful of the tomato mixture and a few sprigs of coriander. Fold the tortillas in half, then half again and serve while still warm with halved limes squeezed over.

GF
If using gluten-free tortillas

AVOCADO

The most popular and notorious fruit of the millennial generation, the creamy avocado is surely worth forfeiting the burden of a huge future mortgage for. Low in sugar for a fruit, avocados are rich in commonly under-eaten nutrients such as dietary fibre, mono-unsaturated fatty acids, vitamins A, C and E, folate and potassium.

Scrambled chickpeas and Breakfast burritos

Potato rosti

I lived and cooked in Switzerland for a while and made rosti for breakfast, lunch and dinner. In the restaurant that I worked in, they shallow-fried the rosti, but I prefer to cook them quite slowly on a low heat, resulting in a super crispy rosti. Cooking slowly will draw the moisture out of the potato so the trick is to keep them a little thick so they don't dry out.

Quick

extra virgin olive oil

4 potatoes, peeled, coarsely grated and excess moisture squeezed out

sea salt and cracked black pepper

Heat a large non-stick frying pan (about 20 cm diameter) over a medium heat. Add a drizzle of olive oil to form a thin film over the base.

While the oil is heating, take a quarter of the grated potato and scatter it over the base of the pan. Use a spatula to shape the rosti as it cooks, so it is round and an even thickness.

Reduce the heat to medium–low, and cook until the underside is golden. Flip rosti using a spatula and continue cooking until golden, about 3–4 minutes each side. If you find that there is not enough oil in the pan during the cooking process, you can add a little more to prevent the rosti from burning.

GF

Place the cooked rosti on paper towels to absorb any excess fat and repeat process to make 3 more rosti.

Rosti are delicious with roast mushrooms (see opposite) or homemade baked beans (see page 34).

Tobie Puttock

Roast mushrooms with thyme and garlic breadcrumbs

When I was working at The River Café in London we roasted whole mushrooms with garlic and thyme and served them with anything from bruschetta to roast lamb. This recipe is super versatile and works at any time of the day, so take it where you will. If you can't get a hold of portobello mushrooms any large mushroom will do. I've used almost every herb when roasting mushrooms but I find thyme to be the all-time perfect match for mushies. If you can't find any, you can swap it out for fresh marjoram for a different flavour altogether – and if you don't have fresh herbs to hand, a little dried thyme or oregano for that hit of flavour will work as well.

Medium

4 large portobello or other large mushrooms, stalks removed if preferred

2 tablespoons olive oil

sea salt and cracked black pepper

⅔ cup (50 g) homemade breadcrumbs (see page 205) or panko breadcrumbs

2 tablespoons fresh thyme leaves

1–2 cloves garlic, crushed

pinch of dried chilli flakes (optional)

Preheat the oven to 200°C. Line a baking tray with baking paper.

Lay the mushrooms gill side up on the lined tray. Drizzle 1 tablespoon olive oil over the mushrooms, and season with salt and pepper. Pop into the preheated oven and bake for 20 minutes.

While the mushrooms are cooking, put the breadcrumbs, thyme, garlic, remaining oil, chilli (if using) and a good pinch of salt and pepper in a medium bowl and toss to combine.

After the mushrooms have been cooking for 20 minutes they should be almost done. Remove from the oven and pack a quarter of the breadcrumb mixture into each mushroom. Return to the oven and bake for 5–10 minutes or until the breadcrumbs are golden and toasted.

GF
If using gluten-free breadcrumbs

Potato rosti and Roast mushrooms with thyme and garlic breadcrumbs

Medium

Homemade baked beans

I've grown up eating baked beans – I think my father imported his love for them from the UK along with his 20-something self, and I of course have adopted the passion for the bean. This recipe doesn't contain sugar or any nasties so it's more or less guilt-free. For a bit of a different version you can interchange the paprika with cardamom. Spooned on toast with sambal, this is one of my all-time favourites.

1 tablespoon olive oil	300 g tomato passata
1 clove garlic, crushed	400 g can cannellini beans, rinsed and drained
pinch of ground cumin	sea salt and cracked black pepper
1 teaspoon smoked paprika	grilled bread, to serve (optional)
1 tablespoon tomato paste (puree)	

Heat the olive oil in a large saucepan over low heat. Add the garlic and cook, stirring often, until softened and without colour. Add the cumin, paprika and tomato paste and continue to cook, stirring, for a further 1–2 minutes.

Add the passata and bring to the boil. Reduce heat and simmer gently for 30 minutes, stirring from time to time. Add the beans and cook for a further 10–15 minutes, stirring from time to time, or until thick.

Season with salt and pepper and you are ready to go.

TIP: These beans freeze well and will keep for up to 2 months. I often make a double batch and freeze single-serve portions in airtight containers.

NON-HAEM IRON

Baked beans are a fantastic iron source because combining the beans with vitamin C-rich tomatoes enhances the absorption of the non-haem iron from the beans. Studies have also shown that when cast iron pans are used for cooking, the mineral transfer from the cookware to the food can significantly increase individuals' non-haem iron levels – so much so that using cast iron pots has been proposed by researchers in countries with large iron-deficient populations.

GF
If you leave out
the grilled bread

**Tobie
Puttock**

Pumpkin, ginger and coriander soup, hemp seeds and cashew cream

Medium

GF

My last book was about healthy cooking and so I had to find a way to make pureed soups taste great without the use of creams. I tried simply leaving them out and was blown away at the flavour: it was so much cleaner and pronounced. This recipe takes on the same ethos but I have added a little cashew cream, which is basically blitzed cashews that have gained a cream-like consistency with the help of a little water. You're going to love it.

2 tablespoons olive oil

1 brown onion, finely chopped

1 leek, finely sliced

1 clove garlic, crushed

2 teaspoons finely grated fresh ginger

½ teaspoon ground coriander

1 teaspoon ground cumin

1 kg Japanese pumpkin (squash), peeled, seeds removed and roughly chopped

1 large sweet potato, peeled and chopped

1 litre vegetable stock or water

sea salt and cracked black pepper

2 tablespoons hemp seeds or pepitas (optional)

extra virgin olive oil

FOR THE CASHEW CREAM

1 cup (150 g) raw cashews, soaked in cold water overnight to soften

sea salt

Heat the olive oil in a large heavy-based saucepan over medium heat. Add the onion and leek and cook, stirring often, for 3–5 minutes or until softened and without colour. Add the garlic, ginger, coriander and cumin and continue to cook for a further minute, stirring.

Add the pumpkin, sweet potato and stock or water and bring to the boil. Reduce heat and simmer, uncovered, for 40 minutes or until the vegetables are completely soft.

Meanwhile, to make the cashew cream, strain cashews and pop into a food processor with ½ cup (125 ml) water and blitz until smooth. Season with salt and adjust the consistency with a little more water if the cream is too thick.

Use a blender, stick blender or food processor to blend soup to a smooth puree, then season to taste with salt and pepper. (If using a food processor or blender, cool the soup slightly before processing and do it in batches.) Return to a clean saucepan and reheat over medium–low heat.

Serve with a swirl of the cashew cream, a scattering of hemp seeds (if using) and a drizzle of your favourite extra virgin olive oil.

TIP: This soup freezes well and keeps for up to 2 months. I like to freeze in single-serve airtight containers.

Broccoli and kale soup

The more I eat healthy food, the more I appreciate simple things. I've always appreciated simplicity in flavour because I focused on Italian cooking for more than 20 years and, for me, Italian cuisine showcases ingredients at their best. This recipe is like that. Because it's not drowned in cream, you can really taste the leek, spinach and parsley – everything is pronounced and it feels a lot more honest to me. If you like, you can use this recipe as a formula of sorts and interchange the greens, like swapping the kale for extra spinach if that's what's in the fridge.

Medium

¼ cup (60 ml) olive oil

1 brown onion, roughly chopped

½ teaspoon dried chilli flakes (optional)

2 celery stalks, roughly chopped

1 large leek, white part only, sliced

3 cloves garlic, roughly sliced

2 litres vegetables stock

2 large heads broccoli (about 800 g), roughly chopped

200 g trimmed kale, roughly chopped (see tip)

100 g baby spinach leaves

small handful (¼ cup) flat-leaf parsley leaves

sea salt and cracked black pepper

GF

Heat the olive oil in a large heavy-based saucepan over medium heat. Add the onion, chilli (if using), celery, leek and garlic and cook, stirring often, for 5 minutes or until soft and without colour.

Add the stock and bring to the boil, then reduce heat to a gentle simmer. Add the broccoli and cook for 5 minutes. Add the kale and cook for a further 5 minutes. Remove from the heat and fold through the spinach and parsley.

Use a blender, stick blender or food processor to blend soup to a smooth puree, then season to taste with salt and pepper. (If using a food processor or blender, cool the soup slightly before processing and do it in batches). Return to a clean saucepan and reheat over medium–low heat. Serve.

TIP: You will need 1 large bunch of kale for 200 g of trimmed kale.

CRUCIFEROUS VEGETABLES

With its two main ingredients hailing from the brassica family, this soup should be on everyone's meal rotation. If you google 'benefits of brassicas', prepare to be overwhelmed by the sheer volume of scientific studies indicating the nutritional superiority of these cruciferous vegetables – including growing evidence that the compounds they contain may be associated with a reduced risk of certain cancers.

Minestrone, risoni and kale pesto

Minestrone in its rawest form is vegetables and water, making it naturally vegan, but there will always be variations including the use of animal products in stocks and so on. In this recipe I keep it simple, allowing the vegetables to do the talking, and the risoni makes it a complete meal. Although here I add kale pesto to this recipe, I also find a good dollop of sambal helps to clear out the sinuses.

(L)

Slow

2 tablespoons olive oil	2 parsnips, peeled and diced
1 brown onion, finely diced	1.5 litres vegetable stock or water
2 carrots, diced	400 g can chopped tomatoes
2 stalks celery, diced	⅓ cup (75 g) risoni
2 cloves garlic, finely sliced	sea salt and cracked black pepper
2 bay leaves	2 tablespoons kale pesto (see page 202)

GF
If using
gluten-free
risoni

Heat the olive oil in a large heavy-based saucepan over medium heat. Add the onion, carrots, celery, garlic, bay leaves and parsnips and cook, stirring often, for 5 minutes or until vegetables have softened.

Add the stock or water and tomatoes and bring to the boil. Reduce heat and simmer gently, partially covered, for 1 hour.

Stir in the risoni and cook until the risoni is tender, about 15 minutes. Season with salt and pepper. Serve topped with a good hit of kale pesto.

**Tobie
Puttock**

Lentil, spinach and sage soup

This soup definitely comes from my roots in Northern Italian kitchens and has an excellent place by the fire during the winter months. As the weather cools I will make batches of soup like this to hibernate in the freezer until needed. If freezing, I always leave the spinach out as it will brown during the freezing and reheating process – but it can simply be chopped and stirred through once the soup is hot.

Medium

2½ tablespoons olive oil

1 brown onion, diced

2 carrots, diced

2 stalks celery, diced

3 cloves garlic, finely sliced

small handful (¼ cup) sage leaves, finely sliced

1 bay leaf

400 g can chopped tomatoes

2 × 400 g cans brown lentils, rinsed and drained

sea salt and cracked black pepper

100 g baby spinach leaves, roughly torn

Heat the olive oil in a large heavy-based saucepan over medium heat. Add the onion, carrots, celery, garlic, sage and bay leaf and cook, stirring often, for 5 minutes or until the vegetables have softened.

GF

Add the tomatoes and 1.5 litres water and bring to the boil. Reduce heat and gently simmer for 30 minutes. Stir through the lentils and continue to simmer for a further 10–15 minutes.

Have a taste and adjust the seasoning with salt and pepper. Pop a little bit of the spinach in each soup bowl and ladle the hot soup over the spinach.

Tobie Puttock

Pumpkin and sweet potato soup with sambal

Now this is a soup that I cook all the time – or to be more accurate, one that I *eat* all the time. I don't actually *cook* it that often because I triple this recipe and freeze it – it freezes beautifully. Having things like this in the fridge or freezer are an absolute must-have in order to eat well and avoid those bad decisions when hunger hits and the fridge is empty!

Medium

¼ cup (60 ml) olive oil

1 brown onion, roughly chopped

3 cloves garlic, thinly sliced

1 teaspoon ground coriander

2 teaspoons ground cumin

500 g sweet potato, peeled and roughly chopped

500 g Japanese pumpkin (squash), peeled, seeds removed and roughly chopped

1.5 litres vegetable stock or water

400 g can chickpeas, rinsed and drained

sea salt and cracked black pepper

sambal, to serve (see page 198)

Heat the olive oil in a large heavy-based saucepan over medium heat. Add the onion, garlic, coriander and cumin and cook, stirring often, for 4–5 minutes or until onion is softened.

Add the sweet potato and pumpkin and continue to cook, stirring often, for a further 5 minutes. Add the stock or water and bring to the boil. Reduce heat and simmer for 30 minutes. Add the chickpeas and simmer for a further 15 minutes.

GF

Use a blender, stick blender or food processor to blend the soup to a smooth puree, then season with salt and pepper. (If using a food processor or blender, cool the soup slightly before processing and do it in batches). Return to a clean saucepan and reheat over medium–low heat. Serve with a healthy dollop of sambal.

TIP: This is healthy food, my friends. You can even roast all of the root vegetables on a big baking tray until golden in colour and then transfer all the ingredients to a pot, top with stock or water and simmer until combined for a deeper flavour.

CHICKPEAS

For such a little legume, chickpeas boast an impressive range of nutrients: fibre, protein and iron as well as potassium, phosphate, calcium, magnesium, zinc, folate, choline and selenium, plus vitamins K, C and B6. They're an absolute staple when consuming a plant-based diet.

Parsnip and leek soup with black pepper breadcrumbs

The parsnips in this recipe take on such a velvety and creamy texture when cooked and pureed. If you are a bit fancy a delicious add-on is truffle oil or fresh truffle, but go easy on it as you don't need much!

Medium

2 tablespoons olive oil	3 cloves garlic, roughly chopped
1 red onion, roughly chopped	4 parsnips, peeled and roughly chopped
1 stalk celery, roughly chopped	2 large leeks, white part only, finely sliced
1 teaspoon dried chilli flakes (optional)	½ cup (35 g) coarse homemade breadcrumbs (see page 205)
1 tablespoon fresh thyme leaves	
2 bay leaves	sea salt and cracked black pepper

GF
If you leave
out the
breadcrumbs

Heat the olive oil in a large heavy-based saucepan over medium–high heat. Add the onion, celery, chilli flakes (if using), thyme, bay leaves and garlic and cook, stirring often, for 5 minutes or until softened. Add the parsnips and leek and continue to cook, stirring often, for a further 5 minutes.

Add 2 litres water and bring to the boil. Reduce heat and simmer gently for about 40 minutes or until the parsnip can be pierced with a small knife.

Meanwhile, pop the coarse breadcrumbs into a mixing bowl and crack in a generous amount of pepper until it can really be tasted.

Once the soup is cooked remove the bay leaves. Use a blender, stick blender or food processor to blend the soup to a smooth puree, then season with salt and pepper. (If using a food processor or blender, cool the soup slightly before processing and do it in batches). You can adjust the consistency by reducing the soup further to thicken it or by adding some more water if it's too thick. Return to a clean saucepan and reheat over medium–low heat.

Serve with a generous sprinkling of the breadcrumbs on top.

PARSNIPS

Parsnips are an awesome low-calorie option because with their high levels of soluble fibre they really help fill you up and may reduce the release of ghrelin, an appetite-stimulating hormone that makes you feel hungry.

Tobie
Puttock

Pea and mint falafel flatbreads

I've always made falafels out of broad beans but when I came up with this version using the ever-accessible frozen pea, my father-in-law uttered the words: 'Oh yes, I will definitely have some more.' So, you guessed it: they're super tasty.

1 cup (120 g) frozen peas

400 g can chickpeas, rinsed, drained and air-dried

pinch of ground coriander

pinch of ground cumin

pinch of baking powder

2–3 cloves garlic, finely chopped

¼ cup (35 g) plain or wholemeal flour

large handful (1 cup) mint leaves

1 tablespoon finely grated lemon zest

sea salt and cracked black pepper

coconut, olive or peanut oil, for frying

TO SERVE

2 vine-ripened tomatoes, roughly chopped

small handful (¼ cup) coriander leaves, finely chopped

1 tablespoon sunflower seeds

sea salt and cracked black pepper

⅓ cup (80 g) chickpea hummus (see page 200)

4 Italian flatbreads (see page 206)

Pop the peas, chickpeas, coriander, cumin, baking powder, garlic, flour, half the mint, lemon zest and a good pinch of salt and pepper into a food processor and pulse until the mixture comes together but still has some texture. Form the mixture into 12 little balls.

Pour enough oil into a large non-stick frying pan until about 3 mm deep, enough to coat the bottom. Heat over medium heat. To test if the oil is hot enough, pop a crumb from the falafel mixture into the oil – it should start to sizzle.

Carefully lower the falafel balls into the oil and cook, turning, for 5 minutes or until evenly browned on all sides. Add a little more oil to the pan if necessary.

Remove with a slotted spoon and transfer to a plate lined with paper towel.

While the falafels are resting, combine the tomatoes, coriander and sunflower seeds in a bowl. Season with salt and pepper and toss to combine.

Smear a generous amount of the hummus onto the flatbreads, top with the warm falafels and finally scatter over the salad and serve.

TIP: It's very important that the chickpeas are completely dry for this recipe. I normally pop mine into a sieve and leave them there for at least a couple of hourse before they are needed.

TIP: The falafel can be shaped however you want, so you could make the mixture into burger patties and cook them on baking paper in a pan with a tablespoon or so of oil. After they are cooked you can remove excess oil with paper towel and then eat or freeze them.

FOOD COMBINING: CHICKPEAS AND GARLIC

The combination of chickpeas and garlic in these falafels is a great way to boost non-haem iron intake. Garlic and onions contain amino acids that are rich in dietary sulfur, an important mineral that our bodies need. These sulfur amino acids have been found to increase the accessibility of iron and zinc in cereals and pulses like chickpeas, especially when cooked.

Pea and mint falafel flatbreads

Medium

Fresh tomato pizza with kale pesto and olives

When I tell my friends that I'm writing a vegan cookbook, most of the time they look at me with an expression that says, 'Wow, that must be hard.' But to be really honest, it's been amazingly easy – vegan food isn't as difficult or restrictive as it might first seem. This recipe is based on something I ate in Italy years ago – I think Italian food really lends itself to the vegan way, as it's all about taking really great ingredients and showcasing them. In this recipe, we're featuring tomatoes that are at their best.

1 × quantity pizza dough (see page 207)

2 tablespoons kale pesto (see page 202)

handful of mixed tomatoes (about 400 g in total), cut into 5 mm thick slices

2 teaspoons fennel seeds, lightly crushed

small handful of green or black olives, pitted and halved

sea salt and cracked black pepper

1 tablespoon hemp seeds, to serve (optional)

extra virgin olive oil, to serve

Preheat the oven to 200°C. Line a rectangular baking tray with baking paper.

Knead the pizza dough on a lightly floured surface a couple of times, then roll it out to form a 28 cm × 15 cm rectangle. Place the rolled-out base onto the prepared tray and using a spoon, smear pesto over it. Scatter with the tomatoes and fennel seeds, followed by the olives, and season with a good pinch of salt and pepper.

Bake for 20 minutes or until browned. Scatter a tablespoon of hemp seeds over the warm pizza, if you wish, and serve with a splash of extra virgin olive oil.

TIP: A mortar and pestle is a great way to crush the fennel seeds.

TIP: This whole pizza can be made and frozen, then defrosted and reheated in the microwave.

HEMP SEEDS

In late 2017, Australia legalised the sale of food products containing hemp – great news, considering that hemp seeds have an excellent nutritional profile and are an environment-ally friendly, pest-resistant crop. Hemp is a complete protein, containing all nine essential amino acids, and is high in fibre, vitamin E and minerals – as well as having a rare optimum ratio of omega-3 and omega-6 fatty acids.

Tobie
Puttock

Eggplant parmigiana

Medium/slow

I've made the traditional version of this dish so many times using so much cheese. It amazes me that when I simply leave the cheese out, rather than trying to substitute it, the veggies stand out strongly. You can really taste the richness of the tomatoes and, to be honest, I prefer this version to the traditional one! Whereas traditionally the eggplants (aubergine) are fried, here we get a fantastic result by grilling them and, as you can imagine, with only a fraction of the oil. Although this is delicious to eat straight out of the oven, it freezes well too.

extra virgin olive oil, for greasing

4 eggplants (aubergine) (about 2 kg in total)

3 cups (750 ml) tomato basil sauce (see page 194)

large handful (1 cup) basil leaves

1 cup (70 g) homemade breadcrumbs (see page 205) or panko breadcrumbs

sea salt and cracked black pepper

1 tablespoon extra virgin olive oil

Preheat the oven to 180°C. Grease a 5 cm deep, 20 cm × 28 cm ovenproof baking dish with a little olive oil.

Use a sharp knife to remove the green end of the eggplants, then cut each eggplant lengthways into 1 cm thick slices.

Preheat a barbecue or grill plate on high. Cook the eggplant slices for 3 minutes each side or until grill marks are visible and the eggplant starts to brown (see tip).

To assemble, spread a fifth of the tomato sauce over the base of the prepared baking dish, then tear 4–5 basil leaves over the sauce. Top with a fifth of the eggplant slices (they don't need to overlap but try not to have big gaps). Spread another fifth of the tomato sauce over the eggplant, followed by some more torn basil leaves, a sprinkling of breadcrumbs and a pinch of salt and pepper.

Repeat the layering, finishing with a layer of eggplant, tomato sauce, basil and finally breadcrumbs. Drizzle with the olive oil and bake for 30–40 minutes, or until the sauce is bubbling.

Set aside for 10 minutes before serving. It will go beautifully with any of the salads elsewhere in this book.

TIP: You can also cook the eggplant slices in a 200°C oven. Place on 2 baking trays and bake for about 10 minutes each side or until browned.

TIP: This dish will keep for up to 2 days in the fridge, covered, or can be frozen for up to 2 months, but be sure to portion before freezing.

**Tobie
Puttock**

Fried tofu sandwich with Japanese barbecue sauce

Sometimes I crave the crispy fried texture of something delicious cooked in oil. Although that's not too often, I don't believe in denying myself if I'm eating well most of the time. So, when the mood hits, this is my meat-free version of the Japanese *katsu sando*, a crumbed and fried piece of chicken or pork slathered in Japanese barbecue sauce. It's quick, satisfying and pairs super well with the cucumber, sesame and chilli salad on page 71 of this book.

Quick

1 cup (250 ml) soy milk

3 teaspoons cornflour (corn starch)

1½ cups (150 g) panko breadcrumbs

¼ cup (35 g) plain flour, for dusting

sea salt

400 g firm tofu, drained and cut into
4 evenly sized pieces

4 tablespoons cottonseed or vegetable oil,
for frying

8 slices white bread

FOR THE BARBECUE SAUCE

½ cup (125 ml) vegan tomato sauce

2 tablespoons soy sauce

1 tablespoon mirin

1 clove garlic, crushed

1 teaspoon finely grated fresh ginger

To make the barbecue sauce, put the tomato sauce, soy sauce, mirin, garlic and ginger in a bowl and stir to combine. Allow to sit while you prepare the remainder of the dish.

Place the soy milk in a shallow bowl and stir in the cornflour until it's dissolved. The result should be the consistency of whisked eggs, although slightly runnier.

Place the breadcrumbs in a second shallow bowl and sprinkle the flour onto a plate. Season with salt. Working one at a time, dust a piece of tofu in the flour, then the soy milk mixture and finally the breadcrumbs, using your hands to really push the crumbs into the tofu. Repeat with remaining tofu.

Heat a large non-stick frying pan over medium–low heat. Cut a piece of baking paper that will fit snugly inside the pan. Lay the baking paper in the base of the pan and then drizzle the oil on top of the baking paper. After 1 minute, carefully lower the tofu into the pan, making sure the pieces are sitting side by side. Cook for 4 minutes each side or until golden. Remove and transfer to a plate lined with paper towel to remove excess oil.

Meanwhile, smear a generous amount of barbecue sauce on each slice of bread. Arrange the 4 pieces of tofu onto 4 slices of bread and top with the remaining slices, giving a gentle push down with the palm of your hand.

Eat and thank me later.

**Tobie
Puttock**

Sweet potato chips with chilli and dill

These are possibly even better eaten cold, as they become really crispy once they cool down after their visit to the oven. I love having these with edamame hummus (see page 201) but they go well with anything really, and are a great low-carb snack. As I often dip these into something, I don't tend to fuss about with the addition of herbs but, if you wish to, a great little touch is to toss them with some finely minced garlic and finely chopped curly leaf parsley right after they come out of the oven.

Slow

2 large sweet potatoes (about 500 g in total), skin on, cut into 5 mm thick slices

2 tablespoons olive oil

sea salt

1 tablespoon finely chopped parsley or dill

½ teaspoon dried chilli flakes

Preheat the oven to 130°C. Line a baking tray with baking paper.

Put the sweet potato slices in a large bowl. Add the olive oil and a good pinch of salt and toss to combine. Place on prepared baking tray and bake for about 1 hour. Turn and cook for another hour or until golden and crisp.

Once cooked, toss the chips with the finely chopped parsley or dill, a pinch of salt and dried chilli flakes.

TIP: The long cooking time of the sweet potatoes will draw out much of the moisture to make them really crispy.

GF

Fig, hazelnut and thyme pizza

So many vegan recipes try to replace or replicate animal-derived ingredients, but for me there is more than enough to play with without having to turn to ingredients produced in a lab. Take figs when they are in season and some of their best friends – acidity in the form of balsamic, thyme and hazelnuts – and you can create one of the most amazing pizzas for brunch, lunch or dinner.

Medium

½ cup (125 g) hazelnut butter (see page 210)

½ × quantity pizza dough (see page 207)

6 fresh figs

1 tablespoon thyme leaves

extra virgin olive oil

balsamic vinegar, for drizzling

cracked black pepper

Preheat the oven to 200°C. Line a pizza tray with baking paper.

Put the hazelnut butter in a bowl and stir in 1–2 tablespoons warm water to make it spreadable.

Knead the pizza dough on a lightly floured surface a couple of times, then roll it out to form a 30 cm circle. Place onto the lined tray and, using a spoon, smear the hazelnut butter over the dough. Tear the figs over the butter. Top with a sprinkling of thyme and a drizzle of extra virgin olive oil.

Bake for 20 minutes or until golden and browned. Serve with a drizzle of balsamic vinegar and some cracked pepper.

Tobie Puttock

Cucumber, hummus and flatbread

Some years ago, we spent a little time in Turkey during the summer. It was really hot and my wife, Georgia, was pregnant. As such we were looking for super clean and fresh food and the place we were staying at had cucumber and hummus available all the time – it was just the freshness we were looking for. This version of that sort of sums up my cooking these days: there's inspiration from travel combined with inspiration from training in kitchens.

1 × quantity Italian flatbread (see page 206)

¼ cup (60 ml) rice vinegar

2 teaspoons pure maple syrup

sea salt

small handful (¼ cup) coriander leaves, coarsely chopped

2 Lebanese (short) cucumbers

1 cup (260 g) chickpea hummus (see page 200)

extra virgin olive oil, for drizzling

pinch of paprika

Prepare the dough as per the Italian flatbread recipe on page 206.

While the dough is resting, put the vinegar, maple syrup, a pinch of salt and the coriander in a large bowl and stir to combine. Use a vegetable peeler to peel ribbons from the cucumbers. Add to the marinade and allow to sit.

Roll out the flatbreads as per the flatbread recipe. Preheat a grill plate or barbecue on high. Cook flatbreads for 1–2 minutes each side or until lightly browned. Once cooked, cut or tear the flatbreads into pieces roughly the size of your palm.

Remove the cucumber from the marinade and arrange on one side of a serving plate, followed by a dollop of hummus and the flatbreads. Serve with a drizzle of oil and a sprinkle of paprika.

Kale, lemon, garlic and seed salad

For a long time, I ate kale with garlic, chilli, lemon and anchovy. I still love that combo so much but now I replicate it vegan-style simply by recreating the saltiness of the anchovy with some very finely chopped capers or olives.

2 cloves garlic, finely chopped	juice of ½ lemon
½ cup (125 ml) extra virgin olive oil	sea salt and cracked black pepper
1 tablespoon salted baby capers, rinsed and roughly chopped	3 cups (300 g) washed and roughly chopped kale
	½ cup (80 g) nut and seed mix (see page 213)

Ⓛ

Quick

Put the garlic, olive oil, capers, lemon juice and a healthy pinch of salt and pepper in a large bowl and whisk with a fork to combine.

Add the chopped kale and nut and seed mix and toss to combine. Taste for seasoning and adjust with salt, pepper and lemon juice as needed.

KALE

You might be wondering if kale really lives up to all the hype, and the honest answer is yes, it does. It's brimming with carotenoids like beta carotene, lutein and zeaxanthin. It has impressive levels of potassium and vitamins A, C and K, and contains more calcium per gram than whole milk. And when you consider that it has enviably high levels of protein for a vegetable and an excellent ratio of omega-3 fatty acids to omega-6, you simply can't deny that in the plant kingdom, this brassica reigns supreme.

GF

Shaved asparagus, pear, walnut and rocket salad

Shaved asparagus is so awesome and yet I find that so many people don't take advantage of owning a vegetable peeler! Forget dragging the spiraliser out of the cupboard: the humble vegetable peeler is so good for making ribbons of zucchini (courgette), beetroot and even melon – as you'll see in some of the salads later in the book. Although we can get asparagus all year round, it is abundant and at its best in spring.

L
Quick

GF

2 bunches asparagus (about 20 spears)

1 brown pear, cored and quartered

handful of baby or standard rocket leaves

½ cup (100 g) walnuts, lightly toasted

FOR THE DRESSING

juice of ½ lemon

2 teaspoons wholegrain mustard

1 tablespoon extra virgin olive oil

sea salt and cracked black pepper

Remove the tough ends of the asparagus. Use a vegetable peeler to peel long ribbons from each asparagus spear.

Slice each pear quarter into 3–4 slices.

To make the dressing, put the lemon juice, mustard, olive oil and a pinch of salt and pepper in a large bowl. Use a fork to whisk to combine.

Add the shaved asparagus, pear and rocket and use your hands to gently combine. Mix through the walnuts and serve.

WALNUTS

Eating walnuts is associated with an epic number of health benefits (unless, of course, you are allergic to nuts!). They're rich in vitamins, minerals and antioxidants and also contain omega-3 fatty acids, which can be difficult to obtain in a plant-based diet. Evidence suggests that walnuts can be helpful for lowering cholesterol, improving artery health, reducing inflammation and supporting brain function. Make sure shelled walnuts have white nut flesh, as if it is yellow this indicates the walnuts are rancid.

Roast pumpkin, freekeh, lime and coriander salad

For 20 years, I've been dressing root vegetables up with oils, herbs, garlic and all sorts. Then one night at home when I didn't have the energy for all that, I put the smallest amount of olive oil on a tray with some pumpkin (squash) and roasted it – and it was seriously the best I have had. And I didn't do anything to it! Pumpkin is really sweet so roasting caramelises the sugars in the pumpkin and it gets all sticky and crispy and . . . oh my, I'm getting emotional now. *Cook this dish.*

Medium

½ Kent pumpkin (squash) (about 1 kg), seeds removed, cut into 4 cm thick wedges

extra virgin olive oil

sea salt and cracked black pepper

2 limes, halved

1 cup (200 g) cooked freekeh

¼ cup (40 g) currants, roughly chopped

½ cup (80 g) nut and seed mix (see page 213)

¼ cup salted baby capers, rinsed

large handful (1 cup) coriander leaves

Preheat the oven to 180°C.

Line 1–2 baking trays with baking paper. Drizzle 1 teaspoon oil over the baking paper and use a piece of pumpkin to smear the oil over the rest of the paper. Add the remaining pumpkin wedges to the lined trays in a single layer. Drizzle a little more oil over the top and season with salt and pepper. Pop the lime halves on the trays alongside the pumpkin. Cook for around 30 minutes, turning the pumpkin at the halfway mark. The pumpkin should be golden and caramelised. If not, roast a little longer.

While the pumpkin is roasting, put the freekeh, currants, nut and seed mix, capers and a pinch of salt and pepper in a large bowl.

Squeeze the juice from the roasted limes into a bowl. Add 2 tablespoons olive oil and a good pinch of salt and pepper, and whisk with a fork to combine.

Once the pumpkin is ready, arrange the pumpkin wedges onto a platter or serving plates. Drizzle a third of the dressing over the warm pumpkin and fold the rest through the freekeh mixture. Scatter the freekeh mixture over the pumpkin and finish by tearing the coriander over the top to serve.

FREEKEH

Freekeh (pronounced 'free-kah') is an amazing grain to use for building satisfying salads as it is both flavoursome and nutritious: it is low GI, low in fat and a good source of protein, iron, calcium and zinc. Freekeh can help provide greater satiety after eating than other grains due to its high fibre levels (twice as much as quinoa and three times as much as brown rice) – and its prebiotic properties are great for feeding our intestinal flora.

Classic coleslaw

In my first job, we made two types of dressing. The first was an emulsion of balsamic and oil and the second was lemon juice and extra virgin olive oil. When I moved to Italy, we dressed everything with lemon juice and extra virgin olive oil. For this recipe, I *was* going to make a creamy dressing using nut butter . . . but tradition got a hold of me. So here we have a light and zingy coleslaw that will be great with almost anything.

Quick

1 tablespoon salted baby capers, rinsed and finely chopped

¼ cup (60 ml) extra virgin olive oil

juice of ½ lemon

sea salt and cracked black pepper

2 cups (160 g) finely shredded red cabbage

1 bulb fennel, trimmed and finely sliced

1 large carrot, shredded

handful (½ cup) flat-leaf parsley leaves, roughly torn

handful (½ cup) mint leaves, roughly torn

½ cup (80 g) nut and seed mix (see page 215) (optional)

GF

Put the capers, olive oil and lemon juice in a large bowl and whisk to combine. Season with salt and pepper.

Add the cabbage, fennel and carrot and toss until evenly coated in the dressing. Taste for seasoning and adjust using salt, pepper and a little more lemon juice if needed.

Fold through the parsley, mint and nut and seed mix (if using) and serve right away.

Cucumber, sesame and chilli salad

This is an amazing dish and so quick to make. I made it one night with the fried tofu sandwich (see page 56) and the two go so well together they should get married.

2 Lebanese (short) cucumbers

1½ tablespoons rice wine vinegar

sea salt

2 teaspoons soy sauce

2 teaspoons toasted sesame seeds

good pinch of dried chilli flakes or chopped fresh chilli (optional)

Quick

Slice the cucumbers in half lengthways and use a teaspoon to remove the seeds and discard. Cut each cucumber into 1 cm thick pieces.

Put the rice wine vinegar, a pinch of salt, soy sauce, sesame seeds and chilli (if using) in a large bowl and use a spoon to mix well.

Add the cucumber to the bowl with the dressing, stir to combine and allow to sit for 5 minutes before serving.

GF
If using
gluten-free
soy sauce

Avocado, sprout and cucumber salad

I love to have this for lunch with a piece of grilled sourdough and a smear of hummus on the side. Amazing.

3 cups (100 g) mixed sprouts like alfalfa or pea	**FOR THE DRESSING**
½ cucumber, thinly sliced diagonally	½ cup (125 ml) extra virgin olive oil
6 radishes, thinly sliced	juice of ½ lemon
sea salt and cracked black pepper	1 tablespoon wholegrain mustard
1 avocado, halved and sliced	
½ cup (80 g) nut and seed mix (see page 213)	

Quick

To make the dressing, put the olive oil, lemon juice and mustard in a small bowl and use a fork to whisk to combine. Add a little more lemon juice if you need more zing in your life.

Put the sprouts, radishes, cucumber and half of the dressing in a large bowl. Season with salt and pepper and gently toss to combine.

Lay the sliced avocado on serving plates and arrange the dressed salad ingredients next to the avocado. Sprinkle with the nut and seed mix and drizzle any remaining dressing over the top. Eat right away.

GF

SPROUTS

Though tiny in size, sprouts are giants of the nutritional realm. Two to seven days from sprouting, these babies contain a higher concentration of nutrients than some other mature plants could ever hope to achieve, so while they're often used in restaurants as a decorative garnish, a lot of the time sprouts probably contain a more diverse range of health benefits than the food they sit on top of! They can also aid digestion thanks to the unusually high levels of enzymes packed inside them. Lots of different varieties of sprouts are available – broccoli, alfalfa, mung bean and more – and they are quite simple to grow at home, making it really easy to incorporate sprouts into many of your meals.

Carrot, chickpea, cumin and mint salad

Let's talk toasted chickpeas – and I'm talking about this here (rather than in the method) simply because it's a nice-to-do but not 100 per cent necessary. If you are in a rush you can make this salad using canned or cooked and strained chickpeas as they are and this becomes a very, very quick salad to make. But if you wish to get them all hot and toasty, preheat the oven to 200°C, scatter the chickpeas over a baking tray and cook until they become golden brown in colour, about 10–15 minutes.

Quick

2 tablespoons extra virgin olive oil	¼ cup (40 g) sultanas, roughly chopped
1 tablespoon apple cider vinegar	1 tablespoon pepitas (pumpkin seeds)
2 teaspoons cumin seeds, dry toasted	sea salt and cracked black pepper
2 large carrots	handful (½ cup) mint leaves
½ cup (100 g) chickpeas, toasted	large handful (1 cup) coriander leaves

GF

Put the olive oil, vinegar and cumin seeds in a large bowl and stir to combine.

Use a vegetable peeler to peel long ribbons from the carrots and pop them into the bowl with the dressing. Now add the chickpeas, sultanas, pepitas and a good pinch of salt and pepper. Toss to combine. Tear in the herbs and toss again before serving.

BETA CAROTENE ABSORPTION

Chickpeas contain phytates, an 'anti-nutrient' which binds to minerals like iron, calcium and zinc in the gastrointestinal tract, making it more difficult for the minerals to be absorbed during digestion. But studies have shown that combining beta carotene–rich foods such as carrot in the same meal can nullify the inhibiting effect of phytic acid – making this recipe both functional and tasty.

Tobie
Puttock

Lentil, mushroom and asparagus salad

I used to make a carpaccio of mushroom when I was living in Italy and really gained an appreciation for this vegetable that, in Australia, is almost always cooked. Saying that, you can cook them if you wish – and the same goes for the asparagus – but I like to celebrate the tastes and textures in their natural glory.

Quick

2 tablespoons extra virgin olive oil

1 tablespoon apple cider vinegar

2 teaspoons Dijon mustard

400 g can lentils, rinsed and drained

2 cups (120 g) button mushrooms, sliced

1 bunch asparagus, ends trimmed and thinly sliced diagonally

60 g baby spinach leaves

sea salt and cracked black pepper

To make the dressing, put the olive oil, apple cider vinegar and mustard in a small bowl and whisk to combine.

Put the lentils, mushrooms and asparagus in a large bowl. Tear in the baby spinach and fold through the dressing. Season to taste with salt and pepper before serving.

GF

BUTTON MUSHROOMS

Probably the least exotic mushroom in the fungi kingdom, white button mushrooms have nevertheless been discovered to contain some extraordinary health benefits. Laboratory studies have indicated that mushrooms may boost immunity and may be associated with protection against certain cancers including breast, prostate and bladder.

**Tobie
Puttock**

Tomato and beetroot salad

Super easy and super awesome. If you're using raw beetroots that need cooking, give them a little scrub, pop them into a saucepan and cover them with water. Bring to the boil and simmer until they can easily be pierced with a knife. Strain, and once cooled remove the skin. When the tomatoes are in season I love to leave them outside for an hour before I'm ready to use them so they can be kissed by the sun. The colours and taste of this salad are amazing – no smoke and mirrors, just good ingredients doing the talking.

Medium

2 large handfuls mixed tomatoes
(about 500 g in total)

2 large cooked and peeled beetroot
(about 160 g in total)

sea salt and cracked black pepper

handful (½ cup) basil leaves

2 tablespoons extra virgin olive oil

1 tablespoon balsamic vinegar

Slice the tomatoes about 5 mm in thickness and do the same for the beetroot.

Arrange the beetroot and tomatoes on a plate and season with salt and pepper. Scatter the basil over the top. Drizzle with the olive oil and balsamic and serve right away.

GF

Tobie
Puttock

Celeriac, radicchio and fennel salad

Now I know not everybody is a fan of aniseed flavours, but if you are then this is a great salad as it takes all of about 5 minutes to make. If making it ahead of time, you can definitely chop the celeriac, radicchio and fennel a little coarser, add in some nut and seed mix (see page 213) and pop it into a plastic container until you're ready to eat – because the vegetables and leaves are fairly robust, they will hold up against wilting once dressed.

Quick

1 bulb baby fennel, fronds picked and reserved	sea salt and cracked black pepper
½ small celeriac, peeled	¼ cup (60 ml) extra virgin olive oil
1 Treviso radicchio, leaves separated	juice of ½ lemon
1 tablespoon salted baby capers, rinsed	handful (½ cup) chervil or flat-leaf parsley leaves

Slice the fennel and the celeriac as finely as you can – this can be done on a mandolin or even with a vegetable peeler.

Put the fennel, celeriac, radicchio, capers, a pinch of salt and pepper, olive oil and lemon juice in a large bowl. Use your hands to carefully fold the ingredients over each other until evenly coated in the dressing. Taste for seasoning and adjust as needed.

GF

Finally, fold through the fennel fronds and the chervil or parsley and serve.

Witlof, apple, radish and walnut salad

We worked with witlof (Belgian endive) a lot in my first job at Caffe e Cucina and then I didn't see it again for years. A relative of endive, radicchio and artichoke, it's available almost everywhere and is a fairly robust salad leaf compared to, say, rocket. It's also great for grilling – in fact, if you happen to be making this as part of a barbecue meal, you can quarter the witlof, grill it until you have char marks visible and then carry on with the recipe.

Quick

GF

1 teaspoon Dijon mustard

2 tablespoons extra virgin olive oil

juice of ½ lemon

sea salt and cracked black pepper

2 witlof (Belgian endives), leaves separated

4 radishes, thinly sliced

1 small red apple, halved, cored and thinly sliced

1 tablespoon roughly chopped tarragon

handful (½ cup) flat-leaf parsley leaves, torn

2 tablespoons walnuts, coarsely chopped

Put the mustard, olive oil, lemon juice and a good pinch of salt and pepper in a large bowl and use a fork to whisk to combine.

Add the witlof, radishes, apple, tarragon, parsley and walnuts to the bowl and use your hands to gently toss to combine. Serve.

Zucchini carpaccio with pine nuts, sultanas and lemon

I first made a zucchini (courgette) carpaccio in the summer of 1999 at The River Café. Until then, carpaccio to me was super thin slices of meat or fish and this vegetable version blew me away. I always think dishes like this are best eaten outside on a sunny day with some fizz, but take that as you will.

Quick

2 zucchini (courgettes) (about 300 g in total)	handful (½ cup) mint leaves
sea salt	1 long red chilli, seeded and thinly sliced diagonally (optional)
2 cloves garlic, thinly sliced	
½ lemon	cracked black pepper
1 tablespoon toasted pine nuts	extra virgin olive oil, for drizzling
1 tablespoon sultanas, roughly chopped	

GF

Trim the ends of both zucchini and use a vegetable peeler to peel long strips from them. Pop the ribbons into a colander with a pinch of salt and toss to combine. Set aside for a few minutes to draw out excess moisture.

Arrange the zucchini on a serving platter with slivers of garlic amongst the zucchini ribbons. Squeeze the lemon over the zucchini and pop the platter into the fridge.

After 30 minutes, the lemon juice will have softened the zucchini. Scatter over the pine nuts, sultanas, mint, chilli (if using) and pepper and finish with a drizzle of olive oil. Serve.

Tobie Puttock

Grilled cos with chilli and almonds

I love this recipe as an example of using slightly unusual yet accessible cooking methods with everyday ingredients. I use almonds for this but you can use any seeds or nuts you wish really.

2 cos lettuces, cut in half lengthways	1 lemon, halved
¼ cup (60 ml) extra virgin olive oil	pinch of dried chilli flakes
sea salt and cracked black pepper	¼ cup (40 g) raw almonds, lightly crushed

Quick

Preheat the barbecue grill on medium–high.

Use a pastry brush (or fingers) to coat the cut surface of the lettuces with 2 tablespoons of the olive oil. Season with salt and pepper.

Put the lettuce on the hot grill and cook for 2–3 minutes, flip and cook for a further 2 minutes or until lightly charred. While the lettuce is cooking, add the lemon halves, flesh side down, and cook for 5 minutes or until flesh is dark and caramel in colour.

Transfer the lettuce and lemon to a serving plate and drizzle with remaining olive oil. Sprinkle over the chilli flakes and crushed almonds. Squeeze that grilled lemon goodness over the lettuce and enjoy.

GF

Shaved fennel, melon and green olive salad

I've been pairing salty and sweet together forever in my restaurant life, normally in the form of prosciutto with melon or figs – so I thought I'd replace one saltiness with another for this one. As olives are brined to soften them, they have a saltiness that's so awesome with melon. Add in the aniseed flavour of the fennel and you've got a legendary salad.

Quick

GF

2 tablespoons extra virgin olive oil

finely grated zest and juice of 1 orange or blood orange

cracked black pepper

pinch of dried chilli flakes (optional)

½ rockmelon (cantaloupe), skin and seeds removed

½ large bulb fennel, fronds reserved

1 orange, peeled and segmented

¼ cup (30 g) pitted green olives, halved

Put the olive oil, 1 teaspoon orange zest, 2 tablespoons orange juice and a good pinch of pepper and chilli (if using) in a large bowl.

Using a mandolin or vegetable peeler, shave thin slices of the melon and fennel. Alternatively, you can use a sharp knife to slice strips as thinly as you can.

Add the melon, fennel, orange segments and olives to the bowl and gently toss to coat with the dressing.

Arrange the salad on a serving plate and scatter the reserved fennel fronds over the salad.

Potato, horseradish and tarragon salad

This is hands down my favourite potato salad recipe, vegan or not. I was going to start concocting a vegan mayonnaise recipe but there are plenty of good ones available to buy these days – so instead let's talk potatoes. It's really important not to boil them as they will cook on the outside and be raw in the middle. A gentle simmer will keep the potatoes intact while cooking them evenly.

Medium

24 small baby (new) potatoes
(about 1 kg in total), scrubbed

sea salt

200 g vegan mayonnaise

2 tablespoons lemon juice

finely grated zest of ½ lemon

1 tablespoon extra virgin olive oil

freshly grated horseradish, to taste

1 small red onion, thinly sliced

1 tablespoon salted baby capers, rinsed

large handful (1 cup) tarragon or dill leaves, roughly chopped

cracked black pepper

2 cups (60 g) pea cress or watercress

GF

Put the potatoes in a pot that's easily large enough to hold them, cover with cold water and add a good pinch of salt. Bring to the boil then reduce to a gentle simmer for 15 minutes or until the potatoes can be pierced with a knife. Drain and set aside to cool a little.

Put the mayonnaise, lemon juice, zest and olive oil in a large bowl and stir to combine. Grate in some horseradish, stir and have a taste. Add a little more as needed.

Add the potatoes to the bowl (I like to halve the larger ones) along with the onion, capers, tarragon or dill and season with salt and pepper. Carefully stir the potatoes through the dressing then fold through the pea cress or watercress and serve.

This salad will keep for a couple of days in the fridge.

HORSERADISH

Not only a tastily potent sinus cleanser, horseradish boasts many of the same health benefits as its brassica family relations such as kale, broccoli and cabbage. Horseradish contains allyl isothiocyanate, a compound produced from cutting or crushing the root, which is currently being studied for its potential anticancer properties. Anti-microbial and gastro-protective effects have also been demonstrated in lab studies.

Tobie
Puttock

Spicy chilli beans

This recipe is sort of what started it all for me. I was playing around with recipes for a food range and decided to make a vegan chilli con carne – and much preferred this version to the classic recipe with beef. That's when I realised the potential of vegan food: not just for humane, environmental reasons, but also because as a chef there is so much flavour to be brought out and enjoyed.

Ⓛ

Medium

2 tablespoons olive oil	400 g can chopped tomatoes
1 brown onion, finely chopped	1 tablespoon tomato paste (puree)
1 red capsicum (pepper), cut into 1 cm pieces	400 g can lentils, rinsed and drained
4 cloves garlic, thinly sliced	400 g can red kidney beans, rinsed and drained
1 tablespoon ground cumin	425 g can black beans, rinsed and drained
1 teaspoon smoked paprika	sea salt and cracked black pepper

GF

Heat the olive oil in a large heavy-based saucepan (cast iron if possible) over medium heat. Add the onion and capsicum and cook, stirring often, for 3–4 minutes, or until softened.

Add the garlic, cumin, paprika, tomatoes, tomato paste and 200 ml water and stir to combine. Bring to the boil, then reduce the heat and simmer gently, stirring occasionally, for 20 minutes.

Add the lentils, kidney beans and black beans and stir to combine. Continue to simmer for 20 minutes to bring the flavours together, stirring from time to time. Add a little extra water if becoming dry.

Taste and season with salt and pepper as needed. I like to serve this with avocado and roasted sweet potato.

TIP: This chilli freezes well and will keep for up to 2 months.

LEGUMES

Blue zones are regions of the world where the inhabitants have the longest life expectancy, often living past 100 years. When assessing the five blue zones, researchers discovered nine particular factors believed to be the key to longevity. One of these factors was consumption of a mostly plant-based diet with a high intake of legumes – and this delicious dish really shows other plant-based recipes how it's done. Aside from containing a great deal of fibre, protein and minerals, the beans and lentils have high levels of non-haem iron and by cooking them with onion, garlic, tomato and capsicum in a cast iron pot, you'll be helping to aid its absorption.

Tobie Puttock

Penne with roasted tomato, garlic and olives

Penne and tomato is my last wish meal. When I lived in Italy we had it every day for lunch, with good olive oil and fresh basil that grew outside the kitchen. This version is interesting because the tomatoes really do take on a different flavour when roasted, giving you this beautiful combo of roasty, caramelised flavours with the salty tones from the olives.

Medium

3 cups (480 g) cherry tomatoes, halved

2–3 cloves garlic, thinly sliced

2 tablespoons extra virgin olive oil

280 g dried penne

1 cup (150 g) green olives, pitted
and roughly chopped

small handful (½ cup) basil leaves

sea salt and cracked black pepper

2 tablespoons nutritional yeast, to serve (optional)

Preheat the oven to 200°C. Line a baking tray with baking paper.

Place the tomatoes and garlic on the lined tray and drizzle with the olive oil. Pop them into the oven for 10 minutes or until the tomatoes are just starting to burst.

Meanwhile, cook the pasta in a large saucepan of lightly salted water following packet instructions.

Once the tomatoes are ready scatter the olives over the hot tomatoes.

Drain the pasta and add to the baking tray with the tomatoes. Tear in the basil and season with salt and pepper, then fold through to combine. Sprinkle with 2 teaspoons nutritional yeast per serving, if using, and serve right away.

GF
If using
gluten-free
pasta

NUTRITIONAL YEAST

Vitamin B12 is produced by microorganisms and is the only essential nutrient that cannot be supplied in adequate levels from a plant-based diet. The best way to obtain B12 without consuming animal products is to eat fortified foods, such as various cereals, soy products, non-dairy milks and nutritional yeast, or to take a supplement. Fortified nutritional yeast has a cheesy, nutty, savoury flavour and works as a great substitute for parmesan, making it an excellent addition to this dish as well as most of the recipes in this section. Aiming for 2–3 micrograms of vitamin B12 per day, consumed throughout the day in small amounts, allows for optimal absorption.

Orecchiette with cauliflower and peppery breadcrumbs

One of the staff made a similar pasta to this when I was working at Fifteen Melbourne, using crème fraîche to thicken the sauce. To get that creaminess without using dairy, I took a great little trick from my last book, *The Chef Gets Healthy,* and simply pureed the vegetables. As a result, you can actually taste the vegetables, and those peppery crumbs go so well and give a beautiful texture.

Medium

1 small head cauliflower (around 500 g)

¼ cup (60 ml) extra virgin olive oil

½ small brown onion, roughly diced

2 cloves garlic, thinly sliced

1 fresh or dried bay leaf

sea salt and cracked black pepper

320 g dried orecchiette or other short pasta

handful (½ cup) flat-leaf parsley, roughly chopped

1 cup (70 g) homemade breadcrumbs
(see page 205)

Remove the stalk and roughly chop the cauliflower.

Heat 1 tablespoon olive oil in a saucepan over medium–low heat. Add the onion and garlic and cook, stirring often, for 2 minutes. Add the bay leaf and cauliflower and cook, stirring, for a further 2 minutes. Add enough water to just cover the ingredients and bring to the boil. Reduce heat to low and gently simmer for 20–30 minutes, or until cauliflower is soft.

Cool slightly then transfer mixture to a food processor and blitz to a puree, then season to taste with salt and pepper.

Meanwhile, cook the pasta in a large saucepan of lightly salted water following packet instructions. Drain the pasta, reserving 1 cup (250 ml) of the pasta cooking liquid.

Meanwhile, put the cauliflower puree into a saucepan large enough to hold it and all the pasta and heat gently over a low heat.

Stir the pasta through the puree and season to taste with salt and pepper. Adjust the consistency if needed with the reserved pasta cooking liquid. Add the chopped parsley and stir to combine.

Add a generous amount of black pepper to the breadcrumbs so you can really taste it. Serve immediately with a generous amount of the peppery breadcrumbs sprinkled over the top along with a drizzle of the remaining olive oil.

Spaghetti with mushrooms, thyme and garlic

I've been making mushroom pasta forever and have always used crème fraiche, butter and cheese. But the more I eat vegan food, the more I'm convinced of its purity on every level: you can actually taste the mushrooms in this dish and it's a naked sort of taste not clouded by fats from animal products. Originally, I made this recipe without the dried mushroom element but it really does add another dimension and depth of flavour.

Quick

25 g dried mushrooms (such as shiitake)

200 ml warm water

2 tablespoons olive oil

1 brown onion, finely chopped

2 cloves garlic, finely chopped

1 teaspoon chopped thyme leaves

500 g mixed mushrooms, finely chopped

2 teaspoons cornflour (corn starch)

320 g dried spaghetti

small handful (¼ cup) finely chopped flat-leaf parsley

1 tablespoon extra virgin olive oil

sea salt and cracked black pepper

GF
If using
gluten-free
spaghetti
and cornflour

Pop the dried mushrooms into a small food processor or spice grinder and blitz to a powder. Transfer powder to a bowl and pour over 100 ml warm water. Stir to combine and set aside for 5–10 minutes.

Heat the olive oil in a large heavy-based saucepan over low heat. Add the onion and cook, stirring from time to time, for 5 minutes or until soft. Add the garlic and thyme and continue to cook, stirring often, for 5 minutes or until fragrant.

Increase the heat to high, add the fresh mushrooms and cook, stirring, until they release their liquid. Bring to a simmer and allow the liquid to reduce, then add the reserved mushroom liquid mixture.

Combine the cornflour and 100 ml warm water in a small bowl, stirring until completely smooth. Add to the mushrooms and continue to simmer and reduce for 5 minutes, or until the sauce has thickened but there is still enough moisture to coat the pasta.

Meanwhile, cook the pasta in the large saucepan of lightly salted water following packet instructions. Drain.

Add the pasta to the pan with the mushroom sauce. Add the parsley and extra virgin olive oil and season with salt and pepper. Use tongs to gently toss the pasta through the sauce. Serve immediately.

**Tobie
Puttock**

Zucchini spaghetti, peas, asparagus and kale pesto

Given I've dedicated more than half of my life to making fresh pasta, I didn't jump on board the hype when zucchini (courgette) noodles hit town. And while I don't believe they *replace* pasta, I do believe they have a place of their own with certain ingredients. If you have the kale pesto (see page 202) ready to go, this is really quick, fresh and won't leave you crawling for the couch feeling bloated!

Quick

½ cup (130 g) kale pesto (see page 202)

1 bunch asparagus, tough ends removed, chopped into 2 cm lengths

1 cup (160 g) frozen peas

4 large zucchini (courgettes) (about 600 g in total)

1 tablespoon extra virgin olive oil, plus extra for drizzling

sea salt and cracked black pepper

handful (½ cup) basil leaves

Pop the pesto into a bowl large enough to hold all the ingredients.

Bring a saucepan of water to the boil and add a good pinch of salt. Add the asparagus and the peas and blanch for 1 minute or until bright green and tender crisp. Drain and refresh in cold water to stop the cooking process. Add to the bowl with the pesto.

Top and tail the zucchini and use a spiraliser to cut long thin strips, about 30 cm in length (see tip).

Heat the olive oil in a large saucepan over high heat. Add the zucchini and cook, gently stirring, for 1 minute or until the zucchini just starts to soften (don't overload the pan, do this in batches if there looks to be too much).

Add the zucchini to the bowl with the pesto and cooked vegetables and use tongs to carefully fold them through the pesto, then season with a little salt and pepper if needed.

Tear over the basil leaves and serve with an extra drizzle of olive oil.

TIP: Spiralisers are available from kitchenware stores. If unavailable, use a vegetable peeler to cut zucchini into thin ribbons, then cut these into strips.

GF

Tobie
Puttock

Stuffed butternut pumpkin with sage, chestnuts and cranberries

I first made this a few years back on my YouTube channel and it was a big hit. At Christmas there's always that conundrum of 'what to feed the vegan' – well, guess what: this is perfect for everyone. It's totally delicious and it makes more sense to me than moulding tofu into a turkey shape! Even though it has that seasonal feel about it, you can of course make it any time – and the herbs and dried fruits can easily be swapped out for similar ingredients.

Slow

1 butternut pumpkin (squash) (about 1.8 kg), washed

2 tablespoons extra virgin olive oil

1 red onion, thinly sliced

3 cloves garlic, finely chopped

2 tablespoons sage leaves, finely sliced

½ cup (90 g) cooked quinoa

½ cup (60 g) walnuts or cooked chestnuts, roughly chopped

¼ cup (35 g) dried cranberries, roughly chopped

good pinch of allspice

sea salt and cracked black pepper

3–4 sprigs rosemary

GF

Preheat the oven to 180°C.

Slice the pumpkin in half lengthways and use a spoon to scrape out the pumpkin seeds and enough of the flesh so you can fit the stuffing in. Reerve flesh.

Heat the olive oil in a large saucepan over medium heat. Add the reserved pumpkin flesh and cook, stirring often, for 3 minutes. Add the onion, garlic and sage, reduce heat to low and cook, stirring from time to time, for a further 10 minutes or until the onion is soft and translucent.

Fold through the quinoa, walnuts or chestnuts, cranberries, allspice and a good pinch of salt and pepper and stir to combine. Remove from the heat and set aside to cool for 10 minutes.

Pack the stuffing into the pumpkin, keeping it as even as possible in both halves. Press the two halves back together and tie them at 5 cm intervals with kitchen string, so they stay together while cooking. Take the rosemary sprigs and thread them through the string on the outside of the pumpkin.

Wrap the pumpkin tightly in foil and place on a baking tray. Bake for 2 hours or until tender (you can test this by pushing a small sharp knife into the thickest part of the pumpkin).

Serve with all the Christmas trimmings and, of course, cranberry sauce.

Serves 4

Slow

GF

Whole roast cauliflower, romesco and avocado

We often eat this at home no matter what the season is. Like many of the recipes in this book, the secret is in the pantry prep. If you have romesco on hand you are simply popping a cauliflower in the oven and slicing some avocado. Dishes like this always amaze me as you will feel satisfied yet as light as a feather when you are finished.

1 large head cauliflower (about 800 g)

1 tablespoon extra virgin olive oil, plus extra for basting and drizzling

sea salt

1 cup (280 g) romesco sauce (see page 192)

½ cup (80 g) toasted slivered almonds

small handful (¼ cup) flat-leaf parsley leaves, roughly chopped

2 avocados, quartered

Preheat the oven to 180°C. Place a small baking dish of hot water in the bottom of the oven to create some steam so the cauliflower stays nice and moist during cooking.

Discard any outer leaves from the cauliflower and use a small sharp knife to cut off the stem and discard.

Give the cauliflower a rinse under cold water, place it core side down on a chopping board and use your hands to rub the entire surface area of the cauliflower with the olive oil and a pinch of salt. Place the cauliflower in a baking dish, core side down, and bake for 1–2 hours, or until golden in colour and tender (it can easily be pierced with a small sharp knife).

I like to baste the cauliflower a couple of times while it's cooking with a little more olive oil to give it a beautiful golden brown colour.

To serve, smear the romesco sauce over the base of a large serving plate and place the roasted cauliflower on top. Finish with the almonds, chopped parsley, the quartered avocados and an extra drizzle of olive oil.

Black bean burger, sriracha, cucumber, coriander and cos

Medium

I've made a lot of different vegetarian and vegan patties before, but for those the strength of the patty has often relied on the cooking. Not this fella: it can be grilled or barbecued with no issues. I recommend making a large batch of the patty mixture and doing the old cook and freeze – you can double the ingredients for the patties and freeze those, then just defrost and build your burgers when you're ready.

1 cup (170 g) cooked black beans (see tip)	½ cup (150 g) vegan mayonnaise
1 cup (170 g) cooked red kidney beans	sriracha chilli sauce, to taste
1 cup (170 g) cooked brown rice	olive oil, for greasing
1 cup (70 g) homemade breadcrumbs (see page 205)	4 of your favourite burger buns, halved
	4 cos lettuce leaves, trimmed
½ teaspoon paprika	½ cucumber, cut into 5 mm thick slices diagonally
½ teaspoon ground cumin	1 avocado, halved and sliced
1 teaspoon soy sauce	large handful (1 cup) coriander leaves
sea salt and cracked black pepper	1 cup alfalfa sprouts

Pop the black beans, kidney beans, rice, breadcrumbs, paprika, cumin, soy sauce and a pinch of salt and pepper into the bowl of a food processor and pulse until you have a breadcrumb consistency. The mixture will be a little crumbly looking.

Using clean hands, shape the mixture into 4 patties, really pressing the mixture together. Place on a plate, cover, and chill in the fridge for 30 minutes.

Combine the mayonnaise and sriracha to taste (I normally put 1 tablespoon sriracha in for this amount of mayonnaise) in a bowl and give it a good stir.

Preheat a barbecue, grill plate or non-stick frying pan on high and lightly grease with olive oil. Cook the patties for 5 minutes on each side, or until browned and warmed through.

Warm the buns on the barbecue or grill or in a preheated oven.

Divide the cos and cucumber between the four bottom halves of the buns and place a patty on top of each. Top the patties with a big dollop of sriracha mayonnaise followed by avocado, coriander, sprouts and bun tops. Eat before someone pinches it from you.

TIP: Canned black beans and red kidney beans work well for this recipe. Make sure you rinse and drain them well before using.

Serves 6–8

Lentil, sweet potato and mushroom shepherd's pie

I grew up eating shepherd's pie, but of the meat variety – and with white potato instead of the lower carb sweet version. This recipe takes a little while but it freezes really well, so when winter is closing in you can make like a bear and prep your pie in advance, ready for hibernation. You may notice that I use both olive oil and also extra virgin olive oil in this recipe. Generally in my kitchen I sauté with olive oil and reserve extra virgin olive oil with its wonderful flavour for salad dressings, folding through purees or even an olive oil chocolate mousse.

Slow

1 tablespoon extra virgin olive oil, plus extra for greasing

1 kg sweet potatoes, peeled and roughly chopped

½ teaspoon grated nutmeg

sea salt and cracked black pepper

2 tablespoons olive oil

1 large brown onion, finely chopped

4 cloves garlic, thinly sliced

2 tablespoons finely chopped rosemary leaves

200 g button mushrooms, quartered

1 tablespoon tomato paste (puree)

200 ml red wine

400 g can chopped tomatoes

400 g can lentils, rinsed and drained

GF

Preheat the oven to 180°C. Grease an 8 cup (2 litre) capacity baking dish with olive oil.

Pop the sweet potatoes into a large saucepan, cover with cold water and add a generous pinch of salt. Place over a high heat and bring to the boil, then reduce heat and simmer for 20 minutes or until tender. Drain. Return potato to same pan and mash with 1 tablespoon extra virgin olive oil until smooth. Add the nutmeg and season to taste with salt and pepper.

Meanwhile, heat the olive oil in a large frying pan over medium–low heat. Add the onion and cook, stirring often, for 8–10 minutes or until soft. Add the garlic, rosemary and mushrooms, increase the heat to medium–high and cook, stirring, for 5 minutes or until mushrooms are golden. Add the tomato paste and cook, stirring, for 2 minutes then add the wine. Simmer until wine has almost evaporated before adding the tomatoes. Bring to the boil then reduce heat and simmer for 10 minutes. Add the lentils and continue to simmer for 10 minutes or until thick. Season to taste with salt and pepper.

Place mixture in prepared dish and top evenly with sweet potato mixture. Bake for 20 minutes or until potato is golden and pie is bubbling. Set aside for 5 minutes before serving with your favourite salad.

TIP: This pie freezes well and will keep for up to 2 months.

110

Tobie
Puttock

SWEET POTATOES

The delicious sweet potato contains more beta carotene, a precursor to vitamin A, than any other vegetable. In fact, 100 grams of cooked sweet potato provides more than 100 per cent of the recommended daily intake of vitamin A. This makes the humble tuber a saviour for non-meat eaters, as vitamin A is essential for healthy growth and development, vision, immunity, skin, teeth and bones – but tends to be more readily obtained from animal products. Because vitamin A is a fat-soluble micronutrient, it is important to consume some fat with the sweet potato, such as the olive oil used in this recipe, to ensure efficient absorption.

Lentil, sweet potato and mushroom shepherd's pie

Braised green beans with cherry tomatoes and paprika

Mum always made these for me when I was little. Once I became a chef I didn't understand why you'd overcook the beans, but given this dish is one of the most cooked recipes in the world, all those people can't be wrong!

Medium

1 tablespoon olive oil	200 g green beans, trimmed
1 red onion, thinly sliced	400 g can cherry tomatoes
4 cloves garlic, finely chopped	sea salt and cracked black pepper
½ teaspoon paprika	handful (½ cup) flat-leaf parsley leaves, roughly chopped
pinch of cayenne pepper	

Heat the oil in a large deep non-stick frying pan over medium heat. Add the onion and cook, stirring often, for 5 minutes or until soft. Add the garlic, paprika and cayenne pepper and continue to cook, stirring, for 2 minutes or until fragrant. Add the green beans and stir to combine.

Add the tomatoes and bring to the boil. Reduce heat and keep at a simmer, stirring from time to time, for 40 minutes or until the sauce has thickened and beans are tender. Season generously with salt and pepper and fold through the parsley. Serve.

GF

**Tobie
Puttock**

Risi e bisi

I remember making this in the late '90s at The River Café and Rose Gray, the co-founder, would continually tell me to make the risotto looser, almost runny, but with a beautiful creamy bind that is a result of the release from the starch into the liquid. Most risotto recipes will use parmesan and butter to achieve the creamy texture but for seafood risotto I have always only ever used an excellent quality cold pressed olive oil plus almost continuous stirring – and in this recipe, I apply the same principle. It works brilliantly.

Medium

1 litre vegetable stock	finely grated zest of ½ lemon
⅓ cup (80 ml) extra virgin olive oil	sea salt and cracked black pepper
3 golden shallots, finely chopped	handful (½ cup) flat-leaf parsley leaves, roughly chopped
2 cloves garlic, finely chopped	
1 cup (200 g) arborio rice	handful (½ cup) mint leaves, roughly chopped
1 cup (160 g) fresh peas (frozen will also work)	

Put the stock in a large saucepan and bring to the boil over high heat. Reduce heat to low and keep the stock at a simmer.

GF

Heat 2 tablespoons olive oil in a large heavy-based saucepan over low heat. Add the shallots and cook, stirring often, for 5 minutes or until soft and translucent.

Add the garlic and rice and continue to cook, stirring, for 3–4 minutes or until grains are well coated in the oil. Gradually add the simmering stock, one ladleful at a time, stirring constantly and making sure the stock is absorbed before you add more. This will take 15–20 minutes; the rice should be al dente yet creamy.

Remove from the heat and add the peas, lemon zest and one final ladle of stock. Stir in the remaining olive oil and a good pinch of salt and pepper. Pop a lid on the pan and set aside for 5 minutes.

Remove the lid and check seasoning. Stir in the herbs and enjoy right away.

Whole roast celeriac with thyme, garlic and black olive sauce

I know that roasting whole root vegetables is fashionable right now, but I don't do it for fashion – I do it because it's a cooking approach that lends itself perfectly to plant-based meals. Take the humble celeriac and, with a little love, it can become the superstar of the table. Of course, you can serve anything with this – the recipe is purely a starting point – but I am a massive fan of the celeriac with the olive sauce as in this recipe. The earthy flavour from the celeriac with the saltiness from the olives is amazing.

Long

GF

1 large celeriac (about 600 g)	6 sprigs thyme
1 tablespoon extra virgin olive oil	4 dried or fresh bay leaves
3 cloves garlic, crushed with your hand or the heel of a knife	sea salt and cracked black pepper
	½ cup (120 g) black olive sauce (see page 190)

Preheat the oven to 180°C

Scrub the celeriac under cold water and remove any fine roots (I use a little brush to do this). Lay down two pieces of foil (one on top of the other) large enough to wrap around the celeriac.

Place the celeriac in the middle of the foil, stalk facing up. Drizzle with the olive oil and crush the garlic, thyme and bay leaves over the top. Season generously with salt and pepper, then wrap in the foil, closing it at the top tightly so the celeriac is wrapped up snugly.

Place on a baking tray and bake for 1½ hours. Carefully open the foil and bake for a further 30 minutes or until golden and tender. To test if cooked, a small knife can easily be inserted into the centre once it is ready; if not, keep cooking.

Slice the cooked celeriac thinly and serve drizzled with black olive sauce.

Over-roasted beetroot with walnut and horseradish cream

This recipe came about purely by accident: one day while writing this book, I was test cooking a few dishes at once and forgot about these beetroot down the back of the oven. When I got them out they were really quite hard on the outside, but once I cut into them the colour and texture blew me away. The outer crust is almost bark-like. I'd never had beetroot like this before, and there's a good chance you won't have either – so give them a go. It's a great way to transform this humble vegetable.

(L)
Slow

4 very large beetroot (about 800 g in total)

2 teaspoons olive oil

sea salt

½ cup (100 g) walnut butter (see page 210)

1–2 teaspoons finely grated fresh horseradish or horseradish cream

2 teaspoons balsamic vinegar

cracked black pepper

extra virgin olive oil, to drizzle

Preheat the oven to 220°C.

Pop the beetroot onto a baking tray, rub them with the olive oil and sprinkle with salt. Bake for 40 minutes or until tender. Continue to bake for a further 20 minutes or until outer skin is crunchy but not burnt.

Meanwhile, combine the walnut butter and horseradish in a bowl. Loosen mixture with a little warm water if too thick. Season with salt.

Remove the beetroot from the oven and set aside to cool. Once cool enough to handle, cut each beetroot in half and smear the balsamic over the cut surface of each half.

Serve the beetroot with the walnut and horseradish cream, a little pinch of salt and pepper and a drizzle of extra virgin olive oil.

GF

Slow-grilled cauliflower steaks with miso, soy, maple and sesame seeds

Medium/Slow

I find many vegan recipes seem to be a sort of pile of braised vegetables but after 20-odd years in kitchens, I am used to having the hero of the plate be a protein of some sort. For me this cauliflower steak ticks that box of providing a centrepiece to the meal. The cauliflower can be cooked in advance, wrapped and kept in the fridge and grilled when you are ready (it will keep for 2 days).

1 cauliflower (about 800 g)	100 ml rice wine vinegar
2 tablespoons sesame oil	1 tablespoon pure maple syrup or brown rice malt syrup
1 tablespoon white sesame seeds	
1 teaspoon black sesame seeds	2 tablespoons olive oil
1 sheet nori	soy sauce, to taste
90 g white miso paste	

GF
If using
gluten-free
miso paste and
soy sauce

Preheat the oven to 160°C.

Trim the stem and any leaves from the cauliflower and discard. Slice the cauliflower into 4 steaks, about 2–3 cm thick. Rub the sesame oil over the cauliflower steaks, being careful not to break them.

Cut 8 pieces of baking paper the same size as the cauliflower steaks and place a piece of paper on both sides of each steak.

Preheat a grill plate or large non-stick frying pan over low heat. Cook the cauliflower steaks, in batches, for 10 minutes, then carefully flip and cook for a further 10 minutes or until tender.

Meanwhile, spread the white and black sesame seeds onto a baking tray and bake for 3 minutes. Add the nori to the tray and continue to cook for a further 1 minute or until the white sesame seeds are golden and the nori is crunchy.

Remove from the oven and pop them into a bowl. Once cool enough to handle, use your hands to crush the nori while combining it with the sesame seeds.

Pop the miso paste, rice wine vinegar, maple syrup and 2½ tablespoons water into a food processor, and process to combine. With the motor running, slowly add the olive oil until the mixture is well combined. Season with soy sauce to taste – I usually use 1–2 teaspoons.

Arrange the cauliflower steaks onto serving plates and top with the dressing. Finish with a super generous sprinkling of the nori and sesame seed mixture.

Tobie Puttock

Mushroom and chestnut wellington

I test cooked this recipe six times, not because it didn't work first time but because it tasted so good that I needed an excuse to make it again and again! Although it might look a little fiddly, it's actually surprisingly simple and definitely has a place at the Christmas table – whether that's for vegans or not.

Slow

500 g baby spinach leaves	sea salt and cracked black pepper
⅓ cup (80 ml) olive oil	350 g (2 sheets) frozen vegan puff pastry, thawed
2 leeks, thinly sliced	plain flour, for dusting
2 tablespoons thyme leaves, chopped	
2 cloves garlic, finely chopped	**'EGG' WASH**
600 g button mushrooms, quartered	½ cup (125 ml) soy milk
250 g peeled cooked chestnuts, roughly chopped	2 teaspoons agave syrup

GF
If using
gluten-free
pastry

Bring a saucepan of water to the boil. Add the spinach and blanch for 1 minute or until bright green, then drain and refresh in cold water to stop the cooking process. Squeeze out as much water from the spinach as possible.

Heat the olive oil in a large heavy-based saucepan over medium heat. Add the leeks and cook, stirring often, for 10–15 minutes or until soft and caramelised. Add the thyme and garlic and cook, stirring, for 2 minutes before adding the mushrooms. Continue to cook, stirring from time to time, for 5 minutes or until mushrooms are golden in colour.

Remove from heat and carefully tip the mixture into a large mixing bowl. Add the spinach and chestnuts and season with salt and pepper. Stir to combine then set aside to cool to room temperature.

Preheat the oven to 180°C. Line a baking tray with baking paper.

Place the sheets of puff pastry on a clean work surface lightly dusted with flour and join them together along their longer edges to make one large rectangle. Spoon the mushroom mixture along one end of the pastry to form an even-shaped log, then carefully roll to enclose the filling in the pastry and join on the underside. Pinch the pastry ends with your fingers to seal the wellington. If you wish you can cut any of the pastry trimmings into leaves or other decorative shapes.

Place the wellington on the lined tray.

To make the 'egg' wash, combine the soy milk and agave syrup in a bowl and brush the wellington with the milk mixture. Bake for 30 minutes or until the pastry is golden and puffed.

Remove from oven and set aside for 5–10 minutes before slicing.

**Tobie
Puttock**

TIP: It's relatively easy to find vegan puff pastry now, and a pastry that's olive oil–based will be vegan.

MUSHROOMS

Mushrooms have been used in Chinese medicine for centuries, so it's no surprise they are packed with nutritional benefits. They're often described as 'meat for vegetarians', and they do contain some iron, but it's the levels of other nutrients in mushrooms that are more impressive: dietary fibre, protein, vitamin D, B complex vitamins and bioactive compounds such as the antioxidants selenium, glutathione and ergothioneine (ERGO). ERGO has recently been studied for its potential on a nutraceutical level, with early research investigating whether it could help combat cellular damage, chronic disease and inflammation. You can expect to hear a lot more about ERGO in the future.

Mushroom and chestnut wellington

Barbecued asparagus with harissa breadcrumbs

After testing this we had it for dinner with some avocado on the side – four times in one week! It's so easy and mega tasty. I barbecue or grill the asparagus but you can also cook them in boiling water, or even roast them in the oven at 200°C until golden. Whichever way you cook them this dish is delicious.

Quick

24 asparagus spears (about 400 g in total), trimmed

2 teaspoons olive oil

2 lemons, halved

½ cup (35 g) homemade breadcrumbs (see page 205) or panko breadcrumbs

1 tablespoon harissa (see page 197)

1 tablespoon finely chopped flat-leaf parsley (optional)

sea salt and cracked black pepper

GF
If using
gluten-free
breadcrumbs

Preheat the grill plate or barbecue on medium.

Toss the asparagus with the olive oil. Put on the hot grill or barbecue and cook for 2 minutes each side or until lightly charred. While the asparagus is cooking, add the lemon halves to the grill, flesh side down, and cook for 5 minutes or until flesh is quite dark in colour and caramelised. Remove and set aside.

Meanwhile, pop the breadcrumbs into a small frying pan over a medium heat and cook, stirring, for 1–2 minutes or until golden. Add the harissa and continue to cook, stirring, until the crumbs are dry and quite dark in colour. Set aside.

Arrange the asparagus between serving plates. Scatter over the parsley (if using) and season with salt and pepper. Sprinkle with the harissa crumbs and serve with the grilled lemon.

TIP: In this recipe I grill the asparagus, but you can also blanch or roast them.

Tobie
Puttock

Barbecued corn with sriracha aioli

Serves 4
as a side

For several years now, I've been making a recipe like this at home using coriander, chilli, lime and parmesan cheese, as well as another variation where I rolled the grilled corn in mayonnaise and then coriander, chilli and parmesan. This vegan-friendly recipe is a little bit of both – plus I get to use my much-loved sriracha sauce and it's super easy to make! While I really recommend trying out my aioli, if you don't fancy making it from scratch and need a little shortcut, simply fold some sriracha through a store-bought vegan mayonnaise instead.

Quick +
soaking time

4 corn cobs, husk intact	**FOR THE SRIRACHA AIOLI**
2 limes, halved	½ cup (75 g) unsalted raw cashews
sea salt and cracked black pepper	2 cloves garlic
pinch of smoked paprika	1 tablespoon olive oil
large handful (1 cup) coriander leaves, roughly chopped	2 teaspoons pure maple syrup
	sea salt
	pinch of cayenne pepper
	pinch of smoked paprika
	sriracha chilli sauce, to taste

GF

To start making the aioli, pop the cashews into a heatproof bowl and cover with hot water. Soak for 1 hour to soften. Drain and set aside.

Preheat the barbecue or grill plate on medium. Put the corn in the husk on the hot barbecue or grill. As the husk starts to char, remove the charred outer layer and place the cob back onto the barbecue until the next layer of husk becomes charred. Repeat this process until you come to the corn itself and cook until the corn kernels are slightly charred.

While the corn is cooking, add the lime halves to the grill, flesh side down, and cook for 5 minutes or until flesh is quite dark in colour and caramelised. Remove and set aside.

Meanwhile, finish making the aioli. Put the cashews, garlic, olive oil, maple syrup, 2½ tablespoons water, a pinch of salt, cayenne pepper and smoked paprika into a blender and blitz on high until smooth. Taste and add sriracha to your liking. I normally add 2 teaspoons, depending on how much heat I'm in the mood for.

Once the corn is charred to perfection, put it into a mixing bowl and season with a pinch of salt, pepper and smoked paprika and add the coriander. Toss to combine. Arrange corn onto a platter with a slashing of the sriracha aioli and the charred lime.

Serves 4
as a side

Medium

GF

Braised eggplant, tomatoes, capers and basil

I learnt to make this dish several years ago while working in London and it's definitely a keeper. Traditionally it's called *melanzane funghetto,* meaning 'eggplant cooked like mushrooms', and the eggplant is dusted in flour and deep-fried before being folded through a tomato and caper sauce. I started roasting the eggplant to make it a little healthier, and guess what: I think it's better.

2 eggplants (aubergine)

⅓ cup (80 ml) olive oil

sea salt and cracked black pepper

1 red onion, thinly sliced

2 cloves garlic, thinly sliced

1 tablespoon pine nuts

400 g can cherry tomatoes

2 tablespoons salted baby capers, rinsed

handful (½ cup) basil leaves, roughly torn

Preheat the oven to 220°C. Line a baking tray with baking paper.

Halve the eggplants lengthways and slice each half into 3 equal-sized pieces. Pop the eggplant into a bowl, drizzle with 2 tablespoons of the olive oil, season with salt and pepper and toss to combine. Place the eggplant on the lined tray and bake for 30–40 minutes, or until browned.

Meanwhile, heat the remaining oil in a small saucepan over medium–low heat. Add the onion and garlic and cook, stirring, for 5 minutes or until the onion softens but is without colour. Add the pine nuts and cook for a further 1–2 minutes or until browned. Add the tomatoes and bring to the boil. Reduce heat and simmer, stirring from time to time, for 20 minutes, or until the tomatoes have broken down and the sauce has thickened.

Add the capers to the sauce, then fold through the roasted eggplant. Continue to cook over a low heat for 10 minutes to allow the flavours to be acquainted, taking care not to break up the eggplant too much. Taste for seasoning and finally fold through the basil.

Serve warm or at room temperature. This goes so nicely with the zucchini carpaccio (see page 84) or the celeriac, radicchio and fennel salad (see page 80) – and if you have leftovers, try tossing it through with some pasta. Amazing stuff.

Tobie
Puttock

Braised zucchini with cherry tomatoes and mint

This recipe is a great example of how vegan food doesn't mean you need to reinvent the wheel in order to eat. It's actually an Italian classic and a variation of the traditional dish *zucchini trifolati*, which sometimes has tomatoes but always has mint and is often served with a piece of chargrilled bread.

Quick

2 large zucchini (courgettes) (about 400 g in total)

1 cup (160 g) cherry tomatoes, halved

1 tablespoon extra virgin olive oil

2 cloves garlic, finely chopped

small handful (¼ cup) mint leaves

sea salt and cracked black pepper

Cut the zucchini in half lengthways and then each half into about 5–6 equal-sized pieces.

Squeeze a few of the seeds out of the halved cherry tomatoes. Heat the olive oil in a saucepan over medium heat. Add the zucchini, stir a little and then leave for 1 minute or so to brown, then keep turning and repeating for a further 5 minutes or until the zucchini is browned.

Add the cherry tomatoes and garlic to the pan, reduce the heat to low and cook for a further 5 minutes or until zucchini is cooked but not mushy. Tear in the mint along with a good pinch of salt and pepper. Gently stir to combine and serve.

GF

Slow-braised fennel, garlic, capers and lemon

When I was working as a chef in Italy we cooked fennel in many ways but in the home kitchen it was always treated simply, and I always respected that. All of the flavours in this recipe are famous friends of the fennel in many cuisines.

Medium

2 large bulbs fennel, trimmed and fronds reserved	1–2 cloves garlic, finely chopped
2 tablespoons extra virgin olive oil	1 tablespoon salted baby capers, rinsed
1 lemon, halved	sea salt and cracked black pepper

Use a sharp knife to quarter each fennel bulb lengthways.

Heat the oil in a large saucepan, big enough to hold the fennel in a single layer, over low–medium heat. Add the fennel and lemon, cut side down, and cook, covered, for 15–20 minutes or until golden on one side. Flip and repeat on the other side until fennel is dark golden and tender. If the pan is becoming dry during the cooking time, lift off the lid and add a tablespoon or so of water to create a little steam and replace lid.

GF

Remove the pan from the heat and squeeze any remaining juice from the lemon over the fennel in the pan, then discard the lemon. Add the garlic, capers and some salt and pepper to the pan and gently turn the fennel to combine, making sure you don't break it up too much.

Serve the fennel with the fennel fronds torn over the top.

Hasselback sweet potatoes

This is my take on the traditional hasselback recipe sans cheese, cream and animal products of any type. I've used sweet potato here as it doesn't stick to your hips as much as the regular super starchy potato!

Medium

12 sage leaves

1 red bird's-eye chilli, seeded and chopped

sea salt

2 cloves garlic, finely chopped

2 tablespoons extra virgin olive oil

4 sweet potatoes (about 600–800 g in total)

1 tablespoon finely chopped flat-leaf parsley

Preheat the oven to 220°C. Line a baking tray with baking paper.

Using a mortar and pestle, pound the sage, chilli and a good pinch of salt together until it resembles a salt consistency (see tip). If the mixture is more like a paste, add a little more salt. Alternately you can use a small food processor and pulse to combine.

Put the garlic and the oil in a small mixing bowl and stir to combine.

Grab a couple of chopsticks and lay them on either side of a sweet potato. Use a sharp knife to make vertical slices through the potato at 5 mm intervals, down to the level of the chopstick, so you're not slicing all the way through. Repeat with remaining sweet potatoes.

GF

Place the sweet potatoes on the lined tray and brush with the garlic oil. Sprinkle with a generous amount of the sage salt mixture. Pop them into the oven and bake for 1 hour or until golden and crisp.

Remove from oven and gently run a fork over the top of the sweet potatoes to expose the grooves of the slices. Serve with another little pinch of sage salt and the chopped parsley.

TIP: I like to make a bigger quantity of the sage salt mixture, as you can always keep it for later. Store in an airtight container for up to 1 month.

Tobie Puttock

Crispy brussels sprouts, parsley and sambal

I wrote a recipe for roasted brussels sprouts in my last book. Since then, I've spent some time in Indonesia filming a cooking show and brought a slight addiction to sambal back with me! For me, the heat of the sambal with the texture of these roasted brussels sprouts is just so moreish – I bet you'll love it too.

Quick

250 g brussels sprouts

2 teaspoons extra virgin olive oil

sea salt and cracked black pepper

½ cup (120 g) sambal (see page 198)

handful (½ cup) flat-leaf parsley leaves, finely chopped

handful (½ cup) mint leaves, finely chopped

GF

Preheat the oven to 180°C. Line a baking tray with baking paper.

Trim the cores of the brussels sprouts, discard any tough outer leaves and then cut each one in half. Place in a large bowl, add the olive oil and a pinch of salt and pepper and toss to combine.

Spread the brussels sprouts over the lined tray in a single layer and roast in the preheated oven for 15 minutes. Carefully add the sambal to the baking tray and stir to coat the sprouts evenly. Roast for a further 5–10 minutes or until browned and crisp.

Return the brussels sprouts to the bowl, toss through the parsley and mint and serve.

BRUSSELS SPROUTS

A cruciferous vegetable, brussels sprouts are not only packed full of nutrients, they are also rich in phytochemicals with cancer-protecting properties, making this recipe a gem as it's delicious – tasting nothing like the boiled horrors from childhood.

Tobie
Puttock

Kale, garlic, shallots, capers and lemon

In my last book, *The Chef Gets Healthy*, I did a recipe not dissimilar to this and my friends continuously send me photos of them making it, because it's quick, delicious and really good for you. Here's the vegan version.

Quick

2 tablespoons extra virgin olive oil

1 small red shallot, finely chopped

2 cloves garlic, finely chopped

1 red bird's-eye chilli, finely chopped (optional)

1 tablespoon salted baby capers, rinsed

500 g kale, tough stalks removed, chopped into 5 cm lengths

juice of ½ lemon

sea salt and cracked black pepper

Heat the oil in a saucepan large enough to hold all the kale (remember it breaks down in size quickly) over a low heat. Add the shallot, garlic and chilli (if using) and cook, stirring, for 5 minutes or until the garlic is soft and without colour.

Add the capers and cook, stirring, for a further 1 minute before adding the kale. Use tongs to turn the kale.

GF

Increase the heat to medium, splash in 1 tablespoon water and pop a lid on the pan. After 2–3 minutes the kale should be starting to soften. Squeeze in the lemon juice and season with salt and pepper. Fold through and serve warm.

Sesame and maple carrots with baba ghanoush

I got the inspiration for this dish when I spotted carrots with sesame on Instagram. They looked amazing and as it happens I had baba ghanoush in the fridge, so I started dipping away and . . . oh my! The smokiness from the baba with the maple and sesame flavours is something else. You're welcome.

Medium

20 baby (Dutch) carrots (about 600 g in total), scrubbed under cold water, unpeeled

1 tablespoon extra virgin olive oil

sea salt and cracked black pepper

2 teaspoons pure maple syrup

1 tablespoon white and black sesame seeds

½ cup (120 g) baba ghanoush (see page 204), to serve

Preheat the oven to 180°C. Line a baking tray with baking paper.

Place carrots on the lined tray. Drizzle with the oil and season with salt and pepper. Pop them into the oven and roast for 20 minutes or until they start to turn golden in colour.

Remove the carrots from the oven and drizzle with the maple syrup, then sprinkle evenly with the sesame seeds. Carefully flip them over so the side with sesame is now facing down on the tray. Roast for a further 15 minutes or until the sesame is golden and toasted. Serve with a dollop of baba ghanoush.

GF

CARROTS

To cook or not to cook? Raw carrots provide higher levels of heat-sensitive B complex vitamins and vitamin C, but cooking carrots enables the release and absorption of greater amounts of beta carotene. As beta carotene is fat-soluble, you can help enhance its absorption by cooking your carrots with a small amount of olive oil. So, in conclusion, a bit of both – raw and cooked – sounds like a win–win scenario!

Roast capsicum, capers, olives, chilli

I'm about to get really deep here, but bear with me: this dish came to me during meditation. Not the grilling part, of course – but the toasty paprika crumbs and plating did for sure. It was a moment of inspiration! I hope you love it, and remember, if it's too spicy, just leave out the chilli.

Medium

3 large red capsicums (peppers)
(about 900 g in total)

½ cup (35 g) homemade breadcrumbs
(see page 205)

1 clove garlic, finely chopped

1 long red chilli, seeded and finely chopped

pinch of paprika

1 tablespoon salted baby capers, rinsed

small handful (¼ cup) flat-leaf parsley leaves,
coarsely chopped

sea salt and cracked black pepper

½ cup (60 g) pitted black olives, roughly chopped

1 tablespoon red wine vinegar

2 tablespoons extra virgin olive oil

GF
If using
gluten-free
breadcrumbs

Preheat the oven to 200°C. Line a baking tray with baking paper.

Place the capsicums on the lined tray and bake for 20 minutes or until the skin is blistered and blackened all over. Remove from oven and use tongs to immediately transfer to a heatproof bowl. Wrap the bowl tightly with plastic wrap and then set aside for 15 minutes. Alternatively, you can cook the capsicums directly over an open flame, or on a hot barbecue or grill plate.

While the capsicums are cooling, pop the breadcrumbs into a small saucepan and cook, stirring, over a medium–low heat until golden. Add the garlic, chilli, paprika and capers and continue to cook, stirring, until the crumbs are dark golden in colour. Fold through the parsley and set aside.

Once the capsicum is cool enough to handle, use your fingers to remove and discard the skin, seeds and core of the capsicums. Avoid doing this under running water, so you hang onto a little extra flavour.

Lay the capsicums directly onto a large plate or platter. Season with a little salt and pepper. Scatter over the olives then drizzle with the vinegar and olive oil. Sprinkle the spicy crumbs over the capsicums and enjoy.

Charred leeks with romesco

My friend Andre introduced me to the joys of charring all kinds of root vegetables and I'm now a big fan. This is a little similar to grilling corn in its husk: the outer layers of the leek burn and the core becomes sweet and soft with a little bit of a smoky flavour.

2 leeks

1 tablespoon extra virgin olive oil, plus extra for drizzling

½ cup (100 g) romesco sauce (see page 192), at room temperature

small handful (¼ cup) flat-leaf parsley leaves, finely chopped

sea salt and cracked black pepper

Medium

Trim the dark green tops from the leeks as well as the very tip of the root. Rub the surface area of the leek with 1 tablespoon olive oil (I use my hands to do this).

Preheat a grill plate or barbecue on medium–high. Cook the leeks for 8 minutes each side or until blackened. Remove and set aside until cool enough to handle. Using your fingers, remove the burnt outer layers of the leeks.

Smear a generous amount of romesco over the serving plate. Peel open the leeks a little and arrange them over the romesco, finishing with a sprinkling of the parsley, a pinch of salt, some cracked pepper and a drizzle of extra virgin olive oil.

GF
If using
gluten-free
bread in the
romesco sauce

Cold spinach with toasted sesame seeds

Did I mention I love Japanese food? For me it's quite similar to Italian food in its approach: take an excellent ingredient and add a few complementary flavours. Spinach itself doesn't have an abundance of flavour but a 20-second dressing makes a massive difference and suddenly we have a toasty, sweet and salt flavour happening that I could eat every day.

Quick

400 g spinach leaves

¼ cup (35 g) toasted white sesame seeds

1 tablespoon soy sauce

2 teaspoons pure maple syrup

Blanch the spinach in a saucepan of boiling salted water for about 3 seconds or until it starts to wilt. Drain in a fine meshed sieve and refresh under cold running water. Cool to room temperature, then squeeze out as much water as you can. Set aside until needed.

Pop the spinach into a mixing bowl with the sesame seeds, soy sauce and maple syrup. Gently stir to combine and serve.

SPINACH

Blanching the spinach in boiling water helps to release its beta carotene content, enabling it to be absorbed more effectively during digestion.

GF
If using
gluten-free
soy sauce

Tobie
Puttock

Mashed potato with lemon and olive oil

Would you believe I wasn't going to put a mashed potatoes recipe in this book? But I realised I had to, and I love this one because it's a little old school/new school with the olive oil as our chosen fat – and if you use a great quality extra virgin olive oil, you'll be eating something out of this world.

1 kg yukon gold or king edward potatoes, peeled and cut into equal sized pieces

6 cloves garlic

¼ cup (60 ml) extra virgin olive oil

¼ cup (60 ml) soy milk or other vegan milk

finely grated zest of 1 lemon

sea salt

Medium

Put the potatoes and garlic into a saucepan, cover with water and add a generous pinch of salt. Bring to the boil then reduce heat and simmer uncovered for 20 minutes or until the potatoes are cooked through.

Drain the potatoes and garlic and return to the same pan. Add the olive oil, soy milk, lemon zest and a pinch of salt and mash until there are zero lumps left. The consistency should be velvety smooth.

Have a taste and adjust the seasoning until you are smiling and going back for more.

GF

Shoestring chips with rosemary and sea salt

I first had these years ago at The Spotted Pig in NYC and thought they were the best. I then popped them on the menu at Fifteen in Melbourne. They're a little naughty, of course – but consider them a once-a-week treat and make up for it with a super healthy dinner the next night!

4 large yukon gold potatoes
(about 600 g in total), peeled

olive oil or coconut oil, for deep-frying

handful (½ cup) rosemary sprigs

sea salt

Quick

Use a mandolin or a knife to cut potatoes into very thin shoestring chips. Sit the cut chips in a bowl of iced water for 10 minutes and then remove and pat dry on paper towel or a clean tea towel. Make sure they are very dry before they hit the oil.

Put enough oil to come halfway up the sides of a deep saucepan, and place over a medium heat. We are looking for a temperature of 175°C and you can either use a thermometer or the old-fashioned way of gently dropping 1 chip into the oil: if it sizzles right away you are ready; if not, wait.

GF

It's best do this in 2 or 3 batches so you don't lower the temperature of the oil too much. Lower the chips into the oil. As they start to turn golden in colour carefully drop the rosemary into the oil as well. Once they are deeply golden in colour remove with a slotted spoon and transfer to a bowl lined with paper towel. Repeat for remaining batches and hit them with an excellent pinch of salt before serving.

Sticky eggplant with miso and sesame

Looking through the recipes in this book, you'll probably notice a big European influence, and that's because I've spent a lot of time working in Europe. But during my down time I like to beeline it to Japan to go snowboarding. As well as the amazing boarding, I also have a huge love for Japanese food – and, now I think about it, most things Japanese. So that explains why there are a few Japanese-inspired dishes in this book! More importantly, though, this one is ridiculously tasty.

Medium

2 eggplants (aubergine)

2 tablespoons olive oil

½ cup (130 g) miso paste

⅓ cup (80 ml) mirin

2 tablespoons (25 g) brown sugar or coconut sugar

2 tablespoons sake

white sesame seeds

Preheat the oven to 220°C. Line a baking tray with baking paper.

Slice each eggplant in half and carefully score the eggplant flesh about 1 cm apart. Rub the olive oil over the entire surface of the eggplant and place, flesh side down, onto the lined tray. Bake for 20 minutes, or until eggplant is tender and golden.

While the eggplant is cooking put the miso paste, mirin, sugar and sake in a small saucepan over low heat and cook, stirring, for 1–2 minutes or until ingredients are well combined.

Once the eggplant is cooked, turn the eggplant over so the flesh side is now facing up and brush the flesh generously with the miso mixture. Return to the oven and bake for 5–8 minutes, or until the sauce starts to caramelise.

Sprinkle the sesame seeds over the top and serve.

Chocolate, date and walnut brownies

This is a rocker of a recipe: it's raw, gluten-free, vegan and damn good. I would rather eat this than a traditional brownie any day of the week.

Quick +
setting time

GF

olive oil, for greasing	**FOR THE GANACHE**
1 cup (100 g) walnuts	½ cup (125 ml) coconut oil
1½ cups (270 g) fresh dates, pitted	½ cup (50 g) raw cacao or Dutch cocoa powder, sifted
½ cup (50 g) raw cacao or Dutch cocoa powder, sifted	¼ cup (60 ml) pure maple syrup
2 teaspoons vanilla extract	sea salt
sea salt	1 teaspoon vanilla extract
¼ cup (30 g) cacao nibs	

Grease a 20 cm square cake tin using a little olive oil, then line the base with baking paper.

Put the walnuts in a food processor and pulse until they resemble fine breadcrumbs. Add the dates and continue to pulse until the dates are finely chopped and the mixture starts to become sticky. Add the cacao, vanilla and a good pinch of salt and pulse to combine.

Transfer mixture to a bowl and stir through the cacao nibs. Using your fingers, press into the lined tin, making sure it's even and there aren't any gaps, holes or air bubbles.

Place in the fridge for about 1 hour or until set and chilled.

Meanwhile, to make the ganache, put the coconut oil into a small saucepan and melt over medium heat. Remove from the heat and whisk in the cacao powder, maple syrup, a pinch of salt and the vanilla until well combined and smooth.

Grab the brownie from the fridge and pour the ganache over the brownie, using a spatula to evenly distribute it. Chill in the freezer or fridge until set.

Use a sharp, preferably hot, knife to slice the brownies into whatever size or shape you like.

TIP: The brownies will keep for up to 1 week in an airtight container in the fridge.

CACAO

Train your taste buds to appreciate the flavour of dark chocolate containing at least 60–70 per cent cacao and enjoy the benefits of this fruit's impressively long list of health benefits. Cacao-rich (70 per cent or higher) dark chocolate is full of flavanols that support cardiovascular health, and research suggests eating small portions is associated with reduced risk of heart attack and strokes, lower blood pressure, increased insulin sensitivity and improved cognitive function.

Tobie
Puttock

Banana fritters with cinnamon and nutmeg

This one is a little bit naughty, but we all need a treat sometimes – and if the oil is at the right temperature, it won't flood the fritters but instead will seal them, making them deliciously crispy on the outside and creamy on the inside.

Quick

4 large very ripe bananas (about 600 g in total), roughly chopped

2 cups (320 g) plain flour

2½ teaspoons baking powder

2 tablespoons brown sugar or coconut sugar

good pinch of ground nutmeg

good pinch of ground cinnamon

1 teaspoon vanilla extract

coconut oil or olive oil, for shallow frying

icing sugar, for dusting

pure maple syrup, for drizzling

GF
If using
gluten-free
plain flour

Pop the bananas in a large bowl and use a fork to mash them really well. Add the flour, baking powder, sugar, nutmeg, cinnamon and vanilla and mix with a wooden spoon until you have a smooth batter.

Pour oil into a large heavy-based saucepan until about 5 cm deep and heat over medium–high heat. (You'll know the oil is the right temperature when a small amount of batter sizzles when added to the oil.)

Once the oil is hot, drop tablespoons of the batter into the oil and fry, in batches, for 4–5 minutes or until golden brown.

Remove fritters with a slotted spoon and transfer to a plate lined with paper towel to remove excess oil.

Serve warm, dusted with icing sugar and a drizzle of maple syrup.

BANANA

Best known for their richness in potassium and fibre, not to mention their flavour and convenience, bananas are having a healthful renaissance since they were discovered to contain significant levels of fructo-oligosaccharides, which function as a prebiotic to feed the healthy gut bacteria essential to our general wellbeing.

Tobie Puttock

Rhubarb and coconut crumble

Whether you are vegan or not, this is good food. Like so many of the dishes I create, I don't aim to make them vegan – they just happen to be vegan. And they also happen to be damn delicious!

Medium

500 g rhubarb (approx. 1 bunch), trimmed and cut into 5 cm lengths

½ cup (125 ml) fresh orange juice

1 teaspoon vanilla essence

2 tablespoons pure maple syrup or brown rice malt syrup

coconut ice-cream, to serve

FOR THE CRUMBLE

1½ cups (135 g) rolled oats

50 g desiccated coconut

1 teaspoon vanilla essence

¼ cup (60 ml) pure maple syrup

finely grated zest of 1 orange

¼ cup (60 ml) coconut oil

100 g raw hazelnuts or walnuts

Preheat the oven to 160°C.

Combine the rhubarb, orange juice, vanilla and maple syrup in an 8 cup (2 litre) capacity baking dish. Bake for 15–20 minutes or until rhubarb is tender.

Meanwhile, put all the crumble ingredients into a food processor and pulse until the mixture resembles coarse breadcrumbs.

Carefully remove baking dish from the oven and scatter the crumble mixture over the top, making sure it's an even thickness. Pop the baking dish back into the oven and bake until the crumble is brown, about 20 minutes.

Serve right away with coconut ice-cream.

Tobie
Puttock

Apple strudel

A lot of the dishes we already know and love happen to be vegan, or only require a few tweaks to get them there. A strudel traditionally requires butter, but I've found that it can be swapped really successfully with olive oil as I've done here in this recipe.

Medium +
resting time

2 cups (300 g) plain flour,
plus extra for dusting

sea salt

2½ tablespoons extra virgin olive oil

200 ml warm water

icing sugar, for dusting

FOR THE FILLING

100 g homemade breadcrumbs (see page 205)

½ cup (70 g) chopped dates

⅓ cup (80 ml) dark rum

6 large granny smith apples (about 1–1.2 kg
in total), peeled

½ cup (60 g) pecans, coarsely chopped

80 g caster sugar

finely grated zest of 1 orange

2 tablespoons orange juice

1 teaspoon ground cinnamon

Put the flour, a pinch of salt, 1 tablespoon olive oil and the warm water in a large bowl and stir with a wooden spoon until the mixture comes together. Once it's too thick to stir, ditch the spoon and use your hands.

Dust a clean work surface with a little extra flour, turn dough out and, using clean hands, knead until smooth and elastic, about 5 minutes.

Drizzle 2 teaspoons olive oil into a bowl, place the dough into the bowl and drizzle the remaining olive oil over the top. Cover with plastic wrap and set aside to rest for about 1 hour.

Meanwhile, to make the filling, put the breadcrumbs into a non-stick frying pan and cook over medium heat, stirring, until dark golden.

Put the dates in a bowl, add the rum and set aside while you prepare the rest of the filling ingredients.

Cut the apples into 5 mm thick slices then place in a bowl with the pecans, sugar, orange zest, juice and cinnamon and mix well.

Preheat the oven to 180°C. Line a baking tray with baking paper.

Dust a clean work surface with flour, then use a rolling pin to roll out the dough as thinly as you can, to about 5 mm thick.

Cover a work bench with a clean tablecloth, then place the dough on the tablecloth in the middle. Very carefully place your fist under the cloth where it's holding the dough, use your other hand to

**Tobie
Puttock**

support the edge of the dough and now drag your fist slowly towards you to stretch out the dough. Repeat this action until you have a very thin, almost paper-thin dough.

Add the dates to the apple mixture and mix thoroughly.

Sprinkle the toasted breadcrumbs over the dough, leaving a 5 cm border. Scatter the apple mixture over the breadcrumbs. Fold the longer edges of the dough in towards the filling and then, starting from the longest end closest to you, use the tablecloth to help roll the strudel up, making sure the ends are sealed. Cut off any excess dough.

Carefully transfer the strudel to the lined tray and bake for 30 minutes, or until pastry is crisp and golden.

Serve dusted with icing sugar.

Apple strudel

Grilled peaches, vanilla, maple and nuts

This is super simple, and sometimes when I make it at home I'll take some nut and seed mix and sprinkle a little over the top to add extra texture. You're going to want vegan yoghurt or ice-cream with this, of course.

Quick/medium

4 freestone peaches, halved and stones removed

1 teaspoon extra virgin olive oil

1 cup (250 ml) white wine

¼ cup (60 ml) pure maple syrup

1 vanilla bean, split lengthways and seeds scraped

50 g seed and nut mix (see page 213)

GF

Preheat the oven to 180°C. Line a shallow baking dish with baking paper. Heat a chargrill pan over low heat.

Use a pastry brush to brush the cut surface of each peach with olive oil. Place peaches, flesh side down, on the chargrill and cook for about 3 minutes. Use a spatula to carefully lift and rotate the peaches 45 degrees, then cook for a further 3 minutes, until the peaches have a lovely lattice pattern of grill marks. Transfer the peaches to the lined dish, cut side up.

Meanwhile, put the wine, maple syrup and vanilla seeds in a small saucepan over medium heat. Bring to the boil then reduce heat and simmer for 1 minute.

Pour the syrup over the hot peaches, then bake for 15–20 minutes or until the peaches are tender.

Serve warm with the syrup, sprinkled with the seed and nut mix.

Tobie Puttock

Banana and berry ice-cream

My daughter, Birdie, LOVES this and I love knowing it's good for her. A quick tip here is to buy a heap of ripe bananas, peel and slice them, and put them into the freezer spread out on a baking tray. When they are completely frozen, bag them into zip-lock bags so they're ready and waiting and you're always primed to make this. Once you have the bananas frozen it's a 2-minute recipe.

2 very ripe bananas

1½ tablespoons coconut milk

2 cups (300 g) mixed fresh berries

pinch of cinnamon

pure maple syrup, to serve

Quick

Peel the bananas, slice them into 1 cm thick rounds and place them side by side on a baking tray. Cover and freeze overnight.

To make the ice-cream pop the frozen bananas and coconut milk in a food processor. Blitz for 1–2 minutes or until smooth, occasionally scraping down the sides of the bowl as needed.

Scoop into bowls and serve straight away with the berries, a sprinkling of cinnamon and a slashing of maple syrup.

GF

Chocolate mousse with berries and pistachios

Aquafaba, the goop that you normally dump after straining out a can of cooked chickpeas, is an amazing ingredient. When you whip aquafaba, it looks exactly like stiff egg whites – the only difference is it doesn't smell like wet dog. Definitely a bonus. So it not only provides a great vegan replacement for eggs, but it also means you're producing less waste from your chickpeas!

Quick + chilling time

160 g fresh raspberries or strawberries, plus extra to serve

½ cup (90 g) coarsely chopped dark vegan chocolate

reserved water from 400 g can of chickpeas (aquafaba)

2 tablespoons pure maple syrup

1 teaspoon vanilla extract

2 tablespoons crushed pistachio kernels

biscotti, to serve

Roughly chop the berries and place in the bottom of 4 × 1 cup (250 ml) capacity serving glasses or bowls.

GF
If using gluten-free biscotti

Melt the chocolate in a heatproof bowl over a saucepan of simmering water (make sure the water doesn't touch the base of the bowl). Set aside to cool.

Meanwhile, put the aquafaba in a large bowl and whisk until you have stiff peaks. Gently fold in the cooled chocolate, maple syrup and vanilla until just combined.

Divide chocolate mixture between the serving glasses. Cover, then pop them in the fridge to chill overnight.

Serve with extra berries, crushed pistachios and biscotti.

AQUAFABA

Aquafaba is a real hero in plant-based cooking because it allows you to replicate many traditional dishes – especially desserts – without sacrificing animals or taste bud enjoyment. A general rule for substitution is 3 tablespoons of aquafaba to replace 1 egg (1 tablespoon is equal to approximately 3–5 calories). Though this recipe uses chickpea water, white bean water also works well. Aquafaba can be stored in the fridge for up to a week or frozen until required, resulting in no food wastage.

Banoffee pie pots

Georgia really wanted me to make a banoffee-inspired recipe and this one is awesome: it has all the roots of the traditional pie without the 14 000 kg of whipped cream, allowing you to actually taste the banana (and still walk after eating it). It's also a great one to prepare in advance for dinner parties where dessert often gets lost after a glass of wine or three.

Quick + setting time

GF

2 bananas, sliced

1 tablespoon shaved vegan chocolate, to serve

FOR THE BASE

1 cup (120 g) pecans

1 cup (100 g) walnuts

1 cup (180 g) pitted Medjool dates

1 tablespoon pure maple syrup
or brown rice malt syrup

MIDDLE LAYER

4 very ripe bananas (about 480 g in total)

⅓ cup (85 g) almond butter (see page 210)

1 tablespoon vanilla extract

CARAMEL LAYER

24 pitted Medjool dates

½ cup (125 g) almond butter (see page 210)

To make the base, put the nuts in a food processor and process until finely chopped. Add the dates and maple syrup and continue to process until the mixture comes together. Press the mixture into the base of a 4 cup (1 litre) capacity serving dish or 4 × 1 cup (250 ml) capacity serving glasses.

To make the middle layer, put the bananas, almond butter and vanilla in a clean food processor and process until smooth. Spread this mixture over the nut base and place in the freezer to set for 20 minutes.

Meanwhile, to make the caramel layer, pop the dates, almond butter and ½ cup (125 ml) water in a clean food processor and blitz until smooth.

Once the pies have set, remove from the fridge and top with the sliced banana. Cover with the caramel layer, sprinkle with shaved chocolate and enjoy.

TIP: Although I think these are better made fresh, they can be constructed into plastic cups and frozen.

Chocolate and salted caramel tart

I've included a chocolate tart in a couple of my previous cookbooks but this one is amazing. I first tested it on a (non-vegan) friend, who pushed a slice into his mouth with great speed and then asked if he could have more. I later told him it was for a vegan book I was writing, to which he said, 'Send me the recipe!' Enough said.

Medium + setting time

GF
If using gluten-free plain flour in the sweet pastry

1 × quantity sweet pastry (see page 208)

sea salt, to serve

SALTED CARAMEL

1 cup (250 g) almond butter (see page 210)

⅔ cup (160 ml) pure maple syrup

⅔ cup (160 ml) coconut oil

1 tablespoon vanilla extract

sea salt

CHOCOLATE GANACHE

280 g vegan chocolate, coarsely chopped

1 cup (250 ml) canned coconut milk

Preheat the oven to 180°C. Roll the pastry out on a lightly floured surface until about 5 mm thick. Press pastry into a 22 cm loose bottomed tart tin, making sure there are no gaps and it is evenly spread.

Place tin on a baking tray, pop into the oven and bake for 10 minutes or until golden around the edges. Set aside to cool.

To make the salted caramel, put the almond butter, maple syrup and coconut oil in a small saucepan over a medium–low heat. Stir with a wooden spoon until the ingredients are melted, well combined and smooth. Remove from the heat, add the vanilla and a good pinch of salt. Have a little taste (be very careful, as it will be hot) and if you can't taste the salt add a little more.

Pour the caramel into the base of the tart case, making sure it's evenly spread, and then place in the fridge or freezer until the caramel is cold and firm to the touch.

To make the chocolate ganache, put the chocolate into a large heatproof bowl and set aside. Heat the coconut milk in a small saucepan over medium heat until almost boiling. Pour the hot milk over the chocolate and allow to sit for 2–3 minutes, then stir with a wooden spoon until the chocolate has melted and the mixture is completely smooth.

Pour the chocolate ganache over the cold caramel and pop into the fridge or freezer until completely set.

Serve with a little extra salt on top if you wish, and maybe some fresh berries.

TIP: The pastry can be supersized and frozen, but not the filling.

Summer pudding

Serves 6–8

When I was working at The River Café, we made this with the most amazing fresh berries and currants, valpolicella wine and sourdough that was brought in on the train from France each morning. I imagine it would have cost a fortune to make, but as it's a simple dessert it really does rely on the quality of the ingredients – so don't skimp on the bread, wine and berries unless you have to.

Slow +
setting time

900 g fresh or frozen mixed berries

½ cup (110 g) caster sugar

1 vanilla bean, split lengthways
and seeds scraped

2 cups (500 ml) red wine (such as valpolicella)

juice of ½ lemon

1 large loaf of sourdough (about 700 g),
crusts removed and cut into 1 cm thick slices

extra fresh berries, to serve

vegan vanilla ice-cream, to serve

If using fresh fruit, wash the fruit in cold water and allow to air dry in a sieve.

Pop the sugar, vanilla seeds and 100 ml water into a large heavy-based saucepan over medium–high heat. Cook, stirring, until the sugar dissolves, then reduce heat to medium and cook, without stirring, until syrup is a light amber colour. Remove from the heat and carefully stir in the red wine.

Add half of the fruit to the pan with the syrup, place the pan over a low heat and stir, being careful not to break the berries. Once the berries have started to release their juices remove from the heat. Add the remaining fruit and the lemon juice and stir to combine. Set aside until needed.

Line a bowl large enough to hold all the ingredients, about 5 cup (1.25 litre) capacity, with plastic film, allowing some overhang. Line the bowl with the sliced bread, being careful not to leave any gaps. Keep aside enough bread to cover the top of the bowl like a lid.

Carefully spoon the berries and their juice into the lined bowl, place the remaining bread on top and fold the overhanging plastic film over the bread to enclose.

Put a plate slightly smaller than the bowl on top of the pudding. Carefully push the plate down to compact ingredients, then wrap the bowl and plate with plastic film to hold the plate down.

Place into the fridge for at least 4 hours or, even better, overnight.

To serve, remove plastic film then invert pudding onto a large serving plate and carefully remove bowl (you may need to use the plastic wrap to pull it out onto the plate). Set pudding aside for 1 hour before cutting into slices.

Serve with extra fresh berries and vegan ice-cream.

Tobie Puttock

BERRIES

Blueberries beat all other fruit – and almost every other food stuff in existence – when measured for antioxidant values in a government review of oxygen radical absorption capacity. In further scientific studies, the compounds within blueberries are being investigated for effects on a slew of age-related diseases, from arthritis and heart disease, to diabetes and Alzheimer's. So don't hesitate to pop them in at every opportunity, and here's a tip: the frozen ones are cheaper and just as nutritious.

Summer pudding

Saffron and cardamom poached pears with cashew cream

I have been poaching fruit my whole career but it wasn't until a few years ago that I stopped adding sugar to the poaching liquid, instead relying on the natural sweetness of the fruit itself. It results in a group of flavours that I think really talk to each other rather than being dominated by an overall sweetness.

Slow

GF

2 teaspoons cardamom pods	2 sprigs thyme
1 cup (250 ml) dry white wine	½ teaspoon saffron threads
½ cup (125 ml) pure maple syrup or brown rice malt syrup	4 firm beurre bosc pears, peeled, halved and cored
1½ tablespoons orange juice	⅓ cup (approx. 80 g) cashew butter (see page 210), to serve

Use a rolling pin to slightly crush the cardamom pods without releasing the seeds.

Put the cardamom, wine, maple syrup, orange juice, thyme, saffron and 1 cup (250 ml) water in a large saucepan and bring to a gentle simmer over a medium heat.

Add the pears and add enough water to just cover the pears. Partially cover the pan and simmer gently for 30 minutes or until pears are tender. Remove pears with a slotted spoon and transfer to a plate.

Bring the poaching liquid to a gentle boil and simmer until reduced by one-third, or until it's nice and syrupy.

Put the cashew butter in a bowl and stir in 2 tablespoons of water to make the consistency smooth and creamy.

Serve the pears with a tablespoon of cashew cream and a drizzle of the syrup.

Tobie Puttock

Serves 4

Roasted pineapple with chilli, mint and maple

Lately I've been seeing photos on Instagram of pineapple roasting over coals in Patagonia, in South Australia . . . basically all over the world. And it's on trend for a reason: it's really, really good. This is pineapple as you've never tasted it before, and it's sure to impress at a dinner party! I've added in a little green chilli here, which I love with the caramelised flavours – it only brings minimal background heat, but feel free to leave it out if you prefer.

Slow + cooling time

1 pineapple (about 900 g)	½ long green chilli, halved (optional)
¼ cup (60 ml) pure maple syrup	1 sprig mint
1 vanilla bean, halved lengthways	

Position a rack in the oven allowing enough room for the pineapple to stand upright while cooking. Preheat the oven to 220°C.

Use a sharp knife to remove the skin and base of the pineapple. If you wish to leave the top on, perhaps wrap the spikes in foil to prevent them from burning.

GF

Put the maple syrup, ½ cup (125 ml) water, vanilla bean, chilli (if using) and mint in a small saucepan over low heat, stirring until all the ingredients are well combined and the liquid is smooth.

Place the pineapple in a baking dish that fits it quite snugly and use a pastry brush to baste some of the maple mixture over the pineapple. Bake for 50 minutes, continuing to baste pineapple every 15 minutes. If the base of the roasting dish becomes dry during this cooking time, add ¼ cup (60 ml) water to the base of the dish.

Once golden and ridiculously delicious-looking, remove pineapple from the oven and set aside to cool for 10 minutes before slicing into 1 cm thick rounds.

Discard the mint and scrape the vanilla seeds into any of the sticky juices that are left in the bottom of the baking dish. If the sticky juices are super thick you can thin with a little water.

Pop the pineapple rounds onto serving plates and drizzle the sticky juices over the top. Dairy-free ice-cream works beautifully with this.

Tobie
Puttock

Slow

Pumpkin and olive oil spice cake

I had my first taste of pumpkin cake on a trip to the US a few years back and was hooked right away. I'm not normally a fan of pumpkin in dessert, but when you're surrounded by snow and it's cold outside, a piece of this goes down so well. As a general rule you don't have to eat this in the snow – it also tastes good on a 40°C day – but, as a favour to me, close your eyes with the first bite and imagine you are standing on the side of a frozen lake watching ice skaters.

olive oil, for greasing

DRY INGREDIENTS

2½ cups (375 g) plain flour

½ cup (100 g) firmly packed brown sugar

1 tablespoon ground cinnamon

1½ teaspoons ground ginger

1½ teaspoons ground nutmeg

1 teaspoon ground allspice

½ teaspoon ground cloves

1 teaspoon baking powder

1 teaspoon bicarbonate of soda

pinch of sea salt

WET INGREDIENTS

1½ cups (375 ml) soy, almond or coconut milk

1 cup (250 g) pumpkin puree

½ cup (125 ml) extra virgin olive oil

2 tablespoons apple cider vinegar

2 teaspoons vanilla extract

FOR THE FROSTING

2 cups (320 g) pure icing sugar, sifted

½ cup (125 ml) extra virgin olive oil

1 teaspoon apple cider vinegar

1 tablespoon vanilla extract

1 tablespoon soy, almond or coconut milk

Preheat the oven to 180°C. Grease a 20 cm springform cake tin with a little olive oil and line the base with baking paper. Grease the paper.

Put the dry ingredients in a large bowl and stir to combine. Combine the wet ingredients in a separate bowl and whisk until smooth and well combined.

Add the wet ingredients to the dry ingredients and stir with a wooden spoon until you have a smooth batter.

Pour the batter into the lined cake tin and bake for 40 minutes or until a skewer inserted into the middle comes out clean. Transfer cake to a wire rack and allow to cool completely before removing from tin.

Meanwhile, to make the frosting, put all the frosting ingredients in the bowl of an electric mixer and beat until thick and fluffy. Alternatively, you can use hand held beaters.

Use a spatula to spread the frosting over the top of the cake and the sides if you wish. Serve.

TIP: This cake will keep for up to 2 days in an airtight container.

Tobie Puttock

OLIVE OIL

As the main source of dietary fat consumed in the Mediterranean diet, olive oil is considered a major factor in studies showing increased longevity and reduced risk of age- and diet-related disease such as Alzheimer's, hypertension, heart attack and stroke for populations in this region. However, not all olive oil is created equally. To take advantage of the health benefits associated with this monounsaturated fatty acid, take care to purchase only extra virgin olive oil. Remember, unrefined and cold-pressed = BEST!

Pumpkin and olive oil spice cake

Rice pudding
and strawberry jam

I grew up eating rice pudding – during winter it's the best. In this recipe, I use a risotto rice for its absorption properties. You can use any dairy-free milk you wish. Soy is my favourite and works a treat.

Quick

¾ cup (150 g) arborio rice

3½ cups (875 ml) dairy-free milk such as soy, almond or coconut

1 vanilla bean, split lengthways

sea salt

1 tablespoon pure maple syrup

⅓ cup (110 g) strawberry or raspberry jam

Put the rice, milk, vanilla bean and a pinch of salt in a saucepan and bring to a gentle simmer over low heat. Continue to simmer, partially covered and stirring from time to time, for 15–20 minutes or until rice is tender.

Once the rice is cooked, remove vanilla bean, scrape out the seeds and return seeds to the rice. Stir through the maple syrup, remove from heat, cover with the lid and allow to stand for 5 minutes. If the rice is very thick you can always add a little extra milk to thin it out.

GF

Serve the rice pudding topped with a dollop of strawberry jam.

Tobie Puttock

Black olive sauce

This sauce has been in my life for years and recently I found a new use for it. My daughter loves olives so much that she picks them out of dishes, so this spreadable sauce makes it a little harder for her to do that! Now, onto the business side of things: marjoram and olives have long had a love affair, but you can of course change the marjoram out for another herb if you'd rather. Although I don't tend to supersize this, you can make a few days' worth to keep you going – but perhaps leave out the herbs as they tend to take on any oil if they spend too much time in the sauce.

Quick

2 cups (320 g) black olives, pitted and coarsely chopped

1 bird's-eye chilli, finely chopped (optional)

1 clove garlic, finely chopped

⅓ cup (80 ml) extra virgin olive oil

1 teaspoon finely chopped marjoram leaves

1 teaspoon finely chopped curly-leaf parsley

cracked black pepper

Put the olives, chilli (if using), garlic and oil in a bowl and stir to combine. Fold through the herbs and season to taste with pepper. Serve right away.

TIP: This sauce will keep for 2 days in an airtight container in the fridge, or without the herbs for a couple of weeks – just add the herbs right before serving.

GF

Tobie Puttock

Romesco sauce

Leave me on a desert island with romesco and I will be happy – that, and good bread. This sauce comes from Catalonia and was originally made by fishermen to eat with fish but it goes with just about everything.

Medium

½ cup (125 ml) extra virgin olive oil, plus extra for greasing

1 large red capsicum (pepper)

3 vine-ripened tomatoes

2 large cloves garlic

½ cup (80 g) almonds, toasted and chopped, plus more to serve

2 thick slices sourdough bread, lightly toasted and torn into pieces

1 teaspoon dried chilli flakes

small handful (¼ cup) flat-leaf parsley leaves, finely chopped

1 teaspoon smoked paprika

sea salt and cracked black pepper

2 tablespoons sherry vinegar

GF
If using gluten-free sourdough bread

Preheat an oven to 200°C. Grease a baking tray using a little olive oil.

Place the capsicum on the greased tray and bake for 15 minutes. Add the tomatoes to the tray and bake for a further 10 minutes or until the skins are quite charred. Remove from the oven and use tongs to immediately transfer the capsicum and tomatoes to 2 separate heatproof bowls. Wrap each bowl super tightly with plastic film and then set aside for 15 minutes to cool.

Use your fingers to remove and discard the skin, seeds and core of the capsicum and tomatoes.

Pop the garlic cloves in the bowl of a food processor and pulse until finely chopped. Add the almonds, bread and chilli and blitz to a paste, scraping down the side of the bowl if needed.

Add the tomatoes, capsicum, parsley, paprika, a pinch of salt and pepper and blitz until smooth. With the motor running, slowly add the vinegar and olive oil in a thin steady stream until you get the consistency you are after. I like mine quite thick so I don't thin it out too much with olive oil. Check seasoning and serve.

TIP: Use right away or use a little and keep the rest in an airtight container for up to 1 week in the fridge.

Tobie
Puttock

Tomato basil sauce

Yes, yes, we've seen this before but I did work in Italian restaurants for 20-odd years so it's an important foundation to many of my recipes! Making this sauce is very easy and always better than store bought. It freezes beautifully, too.

Medium

2 tablespoons olive oil	handful (½ cup) basil leaves
1 brown onion, diced	2 × 400 g cans diced tomatoes
3 cloves garlic, finely chopped	sea salt and cracked black pepper

Heat the olive oil in a medium heavy-based saucepan over medium–low heat. Add the onion, garlic and 2–3 basil leaves and sauté for 10 minutes, stirring from time to time, until the onion is soft and translucent.

Add the tomatoes, increase the heat to medium–high and bring to the boil. Reduce heat to low and gently simmer, stirring from time to time, for 30 minutes or until the sauce has thickened.

Once the sauce is cooked, tear in the remaining basil and fold it through. Season with salt and pepper. Depending on how I'm feeling, I either leave this sauce as is or puree with a stick blender for a silky texture.

GF

TIP: Use right away or allow to cool. The sauce will keep in an airtight container in the fridge for 3–4 days or freeze for up to 2 months.

Tobie Puttock

Chimichurri

In 2012 after I did my last shift in a restaurant kitchen, I started cooking like crazy at home. At first it was awesome for my wife and for me to be eating restaurant-style food at home, but in the end that kind of diet took its toll – enter my book, *The Chef Gets Healthy*. But for a while there I was cooking like crazy and after making several million litres of salsa verde, I welcomed this chimichurri – in some ways the same, but also quite different without the presence of basil and mint.

Quick

3 large handfuls (3 cups) flat-leaf parsley leaves	1 cup (250 ml) extra virgin olive oil
3 cloves garlic	¼ cup (60 ml) red wine vinegar
small handful (¼ cup) oregano leaves	sea salt and cracked black pepper
pinch of dried chilli flakes	

Put the parsley, garlic, oregano and chilli into a food processor and pulse until finely chopped, scraping down the sides of the bowl when needed.

With the motor running, slowly add the olive oil and vinegar and continue to process until the mixture is well combined. Season to taste with salt and pepper.

TIP: This will keep in a jar or airtight container for up to 1 week in the fridge.

GF

Harissa

Oh, harissa, where have you been all my life?! In my 25 years working in Italian kitchens harissa was kept from me. It's now become one of my absolute staples. At home, it has a way of just disappearing – into my mouth on crusty bread, with pasta, in guacamole . . . You get the picture. It's really, *really* good.

12 long red chillies, roughly chopped

6 cloves garlic

1 tablespoon coriander seeds

large handful (1 cup) coriander leaves

½ cup (125 ml) extra virgin olive oil

juice of 1 lemon

sea salt

Quick

Place the chillies, garlic and coriander seeds into a food processor and blitz until finely chopped. Add the coriander leaves and pulse to coarsely chop.

Add the olive oil, lemon juice and salt to taste. Pulse to combine.

TIP: Store harissa in an airtight container or jar for up to 1 week in the fridge.

GF

Sambal

I spent 2 months working on a show in Indonesia and came home with a mild addiction to sambal. Sambal is a complicated recipe in general and there are thousands of different recipes, many using shrimp paste. This, of course, is a vegan version and it's really easy.

Quick

2 tablespoons olive oil

8 long red chillies, roughly chopped

5 red bird's-eye chillies, roughly chopped

8 golden shallots, quartered

1 vine-ripened tomato, quartered

1 clove garlic, peeled

sea salt

1 tablespoon brown sugar

juice of 1 lime

Heat the oil in a medium saucepan over high heat. Add the chillies, shallots, tomato and garlic and cook, stirring often, for 5 minutes or until the tomato starts to break down. Set aside to cool for 5 minutes.

Pop the tomato mixture into the bowl of a food processor and pulse until it forms a thick paste.

Return the mixture to the saucepan over a medium–low heat and cook, stirring, for 5 minutes until the paste turns a dark colour. Season with a good pinch of salt, sugar and lime juice to taste.

GF

TIP: The sambal will keep refrigerated in a clean airtight jar or other container for up to 2 weeks.

Tobie
Puttock

Chickpea hummus

One of the most amazing things happened when I stopped working in kitchens and that was culinary freedom. I worked in Italian kitchens for more than half of my life and we never used paprika or cumin, or made harissa or hummus – but now so many other cooking styles and flavours are opening themselves up to me. Hummus is a great staple to have in the fridge, and when it's made fresh it's a world away from what you'd buy at the supermarket. Have it with raw veggies or in a pita with warm falafel and salad.

Quick

400 g can chickpeas, rinsed and drained	1 tablespoon tahini
good pinch of ground cumin	1 clove garlic, chopped
good pinch of paprika	½ cup (125 ml) extra virgin olive oil
juice of 1 lemon	sea salt and cracked black pepper

Pop the chickpeas, cumin, paprika, lemon juice, tahini and garlic in a food processor and blitz to a puree. Slowly add olive oil until the consistency is smooth and creamy.

Season to taste with salt and pepper and serve.

TIP: This hummus will keep in an airtight container for up to 4 days in the fridge.

GF

Edamame hummus

I came across a recipe many moons ago for edamame hummus and have been making it and tweaking it to arrive at this deliciousness. You should be able to find frozen edamame in the freezer section of most large supermarkets.

1½ cups (220 g) cooked and shelled edamame beans

2 teaspoons white miso paste

¼ cup (70 g) tahini

2 cloves garlic

sea salt

about ½ cup (125 ml) extra virgin olive oil

juice of 1 lemon

1 tablespoon toasted black sesame seeds, to serve

Quick

Pop the edamame, miso, tahini, garlic and a pinch of salt into a food processor and blitz until smooth. Add the olive oil in a slow and steady stream, as you would when making a mayonnaise, until you have the desired consistency. Add the lemon juice to taste and season with a little more salt if needed. Serve topped with sesame seeds.

TIP: This hummus will keep in an airtight container for up to 4 days in the fridge.

Makes 2 cups

Kale and cashew pesto

This recipe is of course different in flavour from the traditional basil pesto, but I have mimicked some of the typical flavours. Cashew nuts, when blended through food, can have a sort of parmesan flavour and they also give a beautiful creaminess.

Quick

3 cloves garlic	juice of 1 lemon
½ cup (75 g) unsalted raw cashews	1½ cups (375 ml) olive oil
3 cups (210 g) packed kale, roughly torn	sea salt

Put the garlic, cashews and kale into a food processor and pulse until finely chopped. Add the lemon juice and olive oil and blitz to combine.

Have a taste and adjust with salt and a little more lemon juice if needed.

TIP: The pesto will keep for up to 1 week in an airtight container in the fridge.

GF

Tobie Puttock

Baba ghanoush

This, my friends, is an important recipe. Have this and other condiments on hand always – maybe for you it's a Sunday thing, make a jar of this and a jar of that. I promise you it will set you up for the week ahead. Some chopped up raw vegetables and baba ghanoush is amazingly tasty and it's super easy to take to work when you're in a hurry.

Medium +
cooling time

2 large eggplants (aubergine)

5 cloves garlic, crushed

½ cup (140 g) tahini

juice of 1 lemon

1 teaspoon ground cumin

sea salt

2 tablespoons extra virgin olive oil, plus extra for drizzling

Preheat the barbecue or grill plate on high.

Pierce the eggplants several times all over with a fork. Put the eggplants on the hot barbecue or grill and cook for 15–20 minutes, or until charred and soft to the touch, turning them from time to time.

Transfer to a plate and set aside to cool.

GF

Once cool enough to handle, remove and discard the ends and skin. Roughly chop the flesh, put into a strainer over a bowl and set aside for 15 minutes to remove excess moisture.

Put the drained eggplant flesh into a bowl and use a fork to mash to a paste. Add the garlic, tahini, lemon juice, cumin, a good pinch of salt and the olive oil and stir to combine. Season with salt and a little extra lemon juice if needed.

Serve at room temperature with a drizzle of extra virgin olive oil over the top.

TIP: This baba ghanoush will keep in an airtight container for up to 1 week in the fridge.

Homemade breadcrumbs

You can use breadcrumbs in numerous recipes to bind, stuff and coat – they're really versatile and handy to have. If you eat bread, chances are you will have leftover end bits. You can pop all the offcuts and leftover bits together and it really doesn't matter if they are from different bread types. This recipe will give you a foundation, and from here you can add spices, herbs, different seasonings – whatever tickles your fancy. Once the breadcrumbs have the moisture removed through the drying process, they should keep in an airtight container for months.

Medium +
cooling time

about 200 g ciabatta bread

Preheat the oven to 120°C.

Tear the bread into roughly equal-sized pieces and place on a large baking tray. Bake for 30–40 minutes or until bread is very crisp and dry. Set aside to completely cool.

Pop cooled bread into a food processor and blitz to desired consistency. I normally keep mine a little coarse.

Italian flatbread

Piadina is a yeast-less flatbread and you can literally make it in 5 minutes. In Emilia Romana in Italy they cook it over charcoal but you can also cook it in a pan. This is a base recipe but sometimes when I'm feeling a little sassy I introduce spices into the dough itself.

Quick +
resting time

2 cups (300 g) plain or wholemeal flour, plus extra for dusting

sea salt

1 tablespoon extra virgin olive oil

½ cup (125 ml) warm water

Sift the flour into a large bowl and make a well in the centre. Sprinkle a pinch of salt into the well and pour in the olive oil and warm water. Mix thoroughly with your fingers until mixture becomes thick and begins to look like dough.

Transfer dough to a lightly floured surface and knead until it's smooth and elastic, about 5 minutes. Put the dough into a clean and lightly oiled bowl, cover with plastic film and set aside to rest for 20 minutes.

Divide the dough into equal-sized pieces (about the size of an egg) and quickly knead each piece into a round ball. Use a rolling pin to roll each ball out to a circle, about 20 cm in diameter and 3 mm thick.

Preheat the barbecue, grill plate or large non-stick frying pan on high. Cook the flatbreads for about 30 seconds on each side or until golden and cooked through. Serve warm.

**Tobie
Puttock**

Basic pizza dough

Even though I've worked mainly in Italian restaurants, believe it or not I haven't made a bunch of pizza during my time in kitchens. The restaurants I've worked in have been a little fancy and not of the pizza-serving type – so for me, pizza has always been something I've made at home.

1 cup (250 ml) tepid water	sea salt
pinch of sugar	1 tablespoon extra virgin olive oil, plus extra for greasing
1 teaspoon dried yeast (½ sachet)	
2¼ cups (350 g) plain flour, plus a little extra for dusting	

Quick +
resting time

Combine the tepid water, sugar and yeast in a small bowl, whisk to combine and set aside for a few minutes.

Put the flour, a pinch of salt and olive oil in a large bowl. Add the yeast mixture and stir to combine.

Use your hands to bring the mixture together into a ball and then turn out onto a floured surface and knead the dough for a few minutes until smooth.

Drizzle a small amount of extra virgin olive oil into a bowl, pop the dough into the bowl and cover with a clean tea towel. Allow to rest for at least 30 minutes or until it's doubled in size.

Sweet pastry

This is an excellent pastry. It isn't quite as short as a traditional sweet pastry and as a result it's quite strong and will benefit from being rolled out quite thinly. The maple syrup in the recipe is purely to sweeten the dough so this can be left out if you wish to use the pastry for a savoury recipe.

Quick +
chilling time

1 cup (120 g) almond meal	⅓ cup (80 ml) coconut oil
2 cups (300 g) plain flour	⅓ cup (80 ml) pure maple syrup
pinch of sea salt	

Pop all the ingredients into a food processor and pulse to combine.

Once the dough has come together, remove from the food processor, shape into a disc and wrap tightly in plastic film.

Place in fridge to chill for 30 minutes before using.

TIP: The pastry can be stored for up to 7 days in the fridge or 2 months in the freezer.

GF
If using gluten-free
plain flour

**Tobie
Puttock**

Caramel sauce

Ladies and gentleman, we have a vegan caramel sauce! This is a base recipe – from here, we can move into the realm of salted caramel with the help of a pinch of Maldon salt, or even a chilli caramel or vanilla caramel. I always keep this in the fridge for drizzling over grilled peaches or using in tarts.

½ cup (160 g) brown rice malt syrup	⅓ cup (80 ml) coconut oil
½ cup (140 g) nut butter (see page 210)	2 teaspoons vanilla extract

Ⓛ
Quick

Put all the ingredients into a small saucepan over low heat and gently whisk until melted and texture is smooth.

Remove and set aside to cool a little before using.

TIP: This sauce will keep in an airtight container for up to 2 weeks in the fridge.

GF

Nut butter

Nut butters play an important part in this book and that's not because I'm just trying to be hip, but because they are super versatile. They can be thinned out using a little bit of warm water and you have a creamy salad dressing. They can also be used in baking and limitless savoury dishes.

Quick

3 cups raw nuts such as macadamias, almonds, cashews, walnuts, hazelnuts or pecans

Preheat oven to 180°C. Line a baking tray with baking paper.

Place the nuts in a single layer on the lined tray and roast for 8–10 minutes or until slightly browned. If you are roasting hazelnuts, wait until they're cooled, then rub them against each other in a tea towel to remove the skins.

Pop the nuts into the bowl of a food processor and process until the mixture is totally smooth and creamy like butter, about 10 minutes. Remove the lid and scrape down the sides every 1–2 minutes during this time.

TIP: The nut butter will keep refrigerated in a clean airtight jar or other container for up to 2 weeks.

GF

Nut and seed mix

Nut and seed mixes are a part of our family's life these days, and for this kind of cooking they add nutrition and texture and really bring simple dishes to life.

50 g pepitas (pumpkin seeds)

50 g sunflower seeds

100 g slivered almonds

100 g pine nuts

100 g raw unsalted cashews, slightly crushed

50 g poppy seeds

Quick

Heat a large heavy-based frying pan over medium heat. Add the seeds and nuts and toast gently, stirring with a wooden spoon so they toast evenly and being careful not to break them, until golden and aromatic.

Remove from the pan and leave to cool completely before storing in a clean airtight container or jar.

TIP: Keep in a cool and dark pantry for several months or in the fridge when the weather is warm.

GF

Further reading

Research studies

- Ahmad, S.F., Koller, D., Bruggraber, S., et al., 'A 1-h time interval between a meal containing iron and consumption of tea attenuates the inhibitory effects on iron absorption: a controlled trial in a cohort of healthy UK women using a stable iron isotope', *Am J Clin Nutr*, 2017, 106(6): 1413–1421. DOI: 10.3945/ajcn.117.161364.

- Atal, C.K., Dubey, R.K., Singh, J., 'Biochemical basis of enhanced drug bioavailability by piperine: evidence that piperine is a potent inhibitor of drug metabolism', *J Pharmacol Exp Ther*, 1985, 232(1): 258–62.

- Chen, S., Oh, S-R., Phung, S., et al., 'Anti-aromatase activity of phytochemicals in white button mushrooms (*Agaricus bisporus*)', *Cancer Res*, 2006, 66(24): 12026–12034. DOI: 10.1158/0008-5472.CAN-06-2206.

- Diego Quintaes, K., Amaya-Farfan, J., Tomazini, F. M., et al., 'Mineral migration and influence of meal preparation in iron cookware on the iron nutritional status of vegetarian students', *Ecology of Food and Nutrition*, 2007, 46(2): 125–141. DOI: 10.1080/03670240701285079.

- Gibson, R.S., Perlas, L., Hotz, C., 'Improving the bioavailability of nutrients in plant foods at a household level', *Proceedings of the Nutrition Society*, 2006, 65(2): 160–8. DOI: 10.1079/PNS200648.

- Jeong, S.C., Koyyalamudi, S.R., Pang, G., 'Dietary intake of *Agaricus bisporus* white button mushroom accelerates salivary immunoglobulin A secretion in healthy volunteers', *Nutrition*, 2012, 28(5): 527–31. DOI: 10.1016/j.nut.2011.08.005.

- Leigh Broadhurst, C., Polansky, M. M., Anderson, R. A., 'Insulin-like biological activity of culinary and medicinal plant aqueous extracts in vitro', *Journal of Agricultural and Food Chemistry*, 2000, 48(3): 849–852. DOI: 10.1021/jf9904517.

- Ngyuen, N, M., Gonda, S., Vasas, G., 'A review on the phytochemical composition and potential medicinal uses of horseradish (*Amoracia rusticana*) root', *Food Reviews International*, 2013, 29(3): 261–275. DOI: 10.1080/87559129.2013.790047.

- Roncero-Ramos, I., Delgado-Andrade, C., 'The beneficial role of edible mushrooms in human health', *Current Opinion in Food Science*, 2017, 14: 122–128. DOI: 10.1016/j.cofs.2017.04.002.

- U.S. Department of Agriculture, Agricultural Research Service, 'USDA Database for the Oxygen Radical Absorbance Capacity (ORAC) of Selected Foods, Release 2', 2010. Nutrient Data Laboratory Home Page: http://www.ars.usda.gov/nutrientdata/orac.

Books

- Bowden, J., *The 150 Healthiest Foods on Earth: The surprising, unbiased truth about what you should eat and why*, Quarto: Massachusetts, 2017.

- Kateman, B., *The Reducetarian Solution: How the surprisingly simple act of reducing the amount of meat in your diet can transform your health and the planet*, Penguin Random House: New York, 2017.

Acknowledgements

I will start this page by thanking my beautiful wife, Georgia, who is 1000 per cent the reason I wrote this book. Georgia started us on the plant-based path at home many years ago and it feels right in every way.

Thank you to Birdie for being you and giving life such purpose. I love you with all my heart and have never laughed as much as when I'm with you. This book is also a result of you, Bird, as Mumma and I wanted you to grow up in a way that's kind and respectful to animals and humans.

As always, I would like to thank my mum, dad and sister Lucy, and my parents-in-law, Bernard and Suzanne Katz, for always being supportive through the good, the bad and the ugly. Massive thanks to Tabitha, Nick, Nancy and the smaller versions of you all (the kids).

Huge thanks to the shoot team: photographer Julie Renouf, stylist Lee Blaylock and Jill Haapaniemi, who kindly assisted. All the team at Penguin Random House: Izzy Yates, Louise Ryan and Adam Laszczuk. And thanks to Daniel New for the amazing design.

Last but not least: my super agents, Bridget and Justine at Chef's Ink.

xxxx

Index

A

aioli (Barbecued corn with sriracha aioli), 129
almond butter, 210
    Banoffee pie pots, 170
    Chocolate and salted caramel tart, 172
almond milk
    Chia, coconut and berry parfaits, 18
    Chocolate chia seed puddings, 21
    Green smoothie formula, 24
    Rice pudding and strawberry jam, 186
almonds
    Grilled cos with chilli and almonds, 87
    Nut butter, 210
    Romesco sauce, 192
    Sweet pastry, 208
almond (slivered)
    Chocolate, cinnamon apricot breakfast bars, 17
    Nut and seed mix, 213
    Whole roast cauliflower, romesco and avocado, 106
appetite-stimulating hormone, 46
apple
    Apple and cinnamon breakfast cookies, 20
    Apple strudel, 160–1
    Green smoothie formula, 24
    Witlof, apple, radish and walnut salad, 82
apricot (dried): Chocolate, cinnamon and apricot breakfast bars, 17
aquafaba
    Chocolate mousse with berries and pistachios, 168
asparagus
    Barbecued asparagus with harissa breadcrumbs, 126
    Lentil, mushroom and asparagus salad, 76
    Shaved asparagus, pear, walnut and rocket salad, 66
    Zucchini spaghetti, peas, asparagus and kale pesto, 102
aubergine *See* eggplant
avocado
    Avocado, sprout and cucumber salad, 73
    Black bean burger, sriracha, cucumber, coriander and cos, 108
    Breakfast burritos, 27
    Green smoothie formula, 24
    nutritional value, 27
    Whole roast cauliflower, romesco and avocado, 106

B

Baba ghanoush, 204
    Sesame with maple carrots with baba ghanoush, 141
banana
    Banana, chia and walnut bread, 14
    Banana, pecan, chia and strawberry pancakes, 23
    Banana and berry ice-cream, 167
    Banana fritters with cinnamon and nutmeg, 156
    Banoffee pie pots, 170
    Green smoothie formula, 24
    nutritional value, 156
Banoffee pie pots, 170
Barbecued asparagus with harissa breadcrumbs, 126
Barbecued corn with sriracha aioli, 129
bars: Chocolate, cinnamon and apricot breakfast bars, 17
basil
    Braised eggplant, tomatoes, capers and basil, 130
    Eggplant parmigiana, 54
    Tomato and beetroot salad, 78
    Tomato basil sauce, 194
beetroot
    Over-roasted beetroot with walnut and horseradish cream, 119
    Tomato and beetroot salad, 78
Belgian endive *See* witlof
berries
    Banana and berry ice-cream, 167
    Chia, coconut and berry parfaits, 18
    Chocolate mousse with berries and pistachios, 168
    Green smoothie formula, 24
    nutritional value, 175
    Summer pudding, 174
beta carotene absorption, 74, 111, 141, 146
black bean
    Black bean burger, sriracha, cucumber, coriander and cos, 108
    Spicy chilli beans, 94
Black olive sauce, 190
blueberry's nutritional value, 175

Black bean burger, sriracha, cucumber, coriander and cos, 108
Breakfast burritos, 27
Green smoothie formula, 24
nutritional value, 27
Whole roast cauliflower, romesco and avocado, 106

Braised eggplant, tomatoes, capers and basil, 130
Braised green beans with cherry tomatoes and paprika, 114
Braised zucchini with cherry tomatoes and mint, 131
breads
    Banana, chia and walnut bread, 14
    Fried tofu sandwich with Japanese barbecue sauce, 56
    Summer pudding, 174
    See also burgers; flatbreads; pizzas
breadcrumbs
    Apple strudel, 160–1
    Barbecued asparagus with harissa breadcrumbs, 126
    Black bean burger, sriracha, cucumber, coriander and cos, 108
    Eggplant parmigiana, 54
    Fried tofu sandwich with Japanese barbecue sauce, 56
    Homemade breadcrumbs, 205
    Orecchiette with cauliflower and peppery breadcrumbs, 99
    Parsnip and leek soup with black pepper breadcrumbs, 46
    Roast capsicum, capers, olives, chilli, 142
    Roast mushrooms with thyme and garlic breadcrumbs, 31
Breakfast burritos, 27
broccoli: Broccoli and kale soup, 41
brownie: Chocolate, date and walnut brownies, 154
brown rice: Black bean burger, sriracha, cucumber, coriander and cos, 108
brussels sprout: Crispy brussels sprouts, parsley and sambal, 136
burgers: Black bean burger, sriracha, cucumber, coriander and cos, 108
burritos: Breakfast burritos, 27

C

cabbage: Classic coleslaw, 70
cacao
    Chocolate, date and walnut brownies, 154
    Chocolate chia seed puddings, 21
    nutritional value, 154
cakes: Pumpkin and olive oil spice cake, 182
cannellini bean: Homemade baked beans, 34
capers (salted)
    Braised eggplant, tomatoes, capers

and basil, 130
Kale, garlic, shallots, capers and
lemon, 138
Roast capsicum, capers, olives,
chilli, 142
Slow-braised fennel, garlic, capers
and lemon, 132
capsicum
Roast capsicum, capers, olives,
chilli, 142
Romesco sauce, 192
Caramel sauce, 209
cardamom: Saffron and cardamom
poached pears with cashew cream, 178
carrot
Carrot, chickpea, cumin and mint
salad, 74
nutritional value, 141
Sesame with maple carrots with baba
ghanoush, 141
cashew
Kale and cashew pesto, 202
Nut and seed mix, 213
Nut butter, 210
Pumpkin, ginger and coriander soup,
hemp seeds and cashew cream, 38
Saffron and cardamom poached
pears with cashew cream, 178
sriracha aioli, 129
cast iron pots, 34
cauliflower
Orecchiette with cauliflower and
peppery breadcrumbs, 99
Slow-grilled cauliflower steaks with
miso, soy, maple and sesame
seeds, 120
Whole roast cauliflower, romesco and
avocado, 106
celeriac
Celeriac, radicchio and fennel
salad, 81
Whole roast celeriac with thyme, garlic
and black olive sauce, 116
Charred leeks with romesco, 145
chestnut
Mushroom and chestnut
wellington, 122–3
Stuffed butternut pumpkin with sage,
chestnuts and cranberries, 105
chia seeds
Banana, chia and walnut bread, 14
Banana, pecan, chia and strawberry
pancakes, 23
Chia, coconut and berry parfaits, 18
Chocolate, cinnamon and apricot
breakfast bars, 17
Chocolate chia seed puddings, 21

nutritional value, 14
chickpea
Breakfast burritos, 27
Carrot, chickpea, cumin and mint
salad, 74
Chickpea hummus, 200
Cucumber, hummus and flatbread, 62
nutritional value, 45, 49, 74
Pea and mint falafel flatbreads, 48–9
Pumpkin and sweet potato soup with
sambal, 45
Scrambled chickpeas, 26
See also aquafaba
chilli
Cucumber, sesame and chilli
salad, 71
Grilled cos with chilli and almonds, 87
Harissa, 197
Roast capsicum, capers, olives,
chilli, 142
Roasted pineapple with chilli, mint and
maple, 180
Sambal, 198
Spicy chilli beans, 94
Sweet potato chips with chili and
dill, 59
Chimichurri, 195
Chocolate, cinnamon and apricot
breakfast bars, 17
Chocolate, date and walnut
brownies, 154
Chocolate and salted caramel tart, 172
Chocolate chia seed puddings, 21
Chocolate mousse with berries and
pistachios, 168
chocolate's nutritional value, 154
See also cacao
cinnamon
Apple and cinnamon breakfast
cookies, 20
Banana fritters with cinnamon and
nutmeg, 156
Chocolate, cinnamon and apricot
breakfast bars, 17
nutritional value, 20
Classic coleslaw, 70
cocoa See cacao
coconut (dried)
Chia, coconut and berry parfaits, 18
Rhubarb and coconut crumble, 158
coconut milk
Chocolate and salted caramel
tart, 172
Rice pudding and strawberry jam, 186
Cold spinach with toasted sesame
seeds, 146
cookies: Apple and cinnamon breakfast

cookies, 20
coriander (leaf)
Barbecued corn with sriracha
aioli, 129
Black bean burger, sriracha,
cucumber, coriander and cos, 108
Breakfast burritos, 27
Carrot, chickpea, cumin and mint
salad, 74
Harissa, 197
Roast pumpkin, freekeh, lime and
coriander salad, 69
coriander: Pumpkin, ginger and
coriander soup, hemp seeds and
cashew cream, 38
corn: Barbecued corn with sriracha
aioli, 129
courgette See zucchini
cranberries: Stuffed butternut pumpkin
with sage, chestnuts and
cranberries, 105
Crispy brussels sprouts, parsley and
sambal, 136
cruciferous vegetables' nutritional
value, 41, 136
crumble: Rhubarb and coconut
crumble, 158
cucumber
Avocado, sprout and cucumber
salad, 73
Black bean burger, sriracha,
cucumber, coriander and cos, 108
Cucumber, hummus and flatbread, 62
Cucumber, sesame and chilli
salad, 71
cumin: Carrot, chickpea, cumin and mint
salad, 74

D

dates
Apple strudel, 160–1
Banoffee pie pots, 170
Chocolate, date and walnut
brownies, 154
dill: Sweet potato chips with chilli and
dill, 59
dips
Baba ghanoush, 204
Chickpea hummus, 200
Cucumber, hummus and flatbread, 62
Edamame hummus, 201
Kale and cashew pesto, 202
dressings for salads, 66, 73

E

Edamame hummus, 201
egg substitute in desserts, 168
eggplant
  Baba ghanoush, 204
  Braised eggplant, tomatoes, capers
  and basil, 130
  Eggplant parmigiana, 54
  Sesame with maple carrots with baba
  ghanoush, 141
  Sticky eggplant with miso and
  sesame, 150

F

fennel
  Celeriac, radicchio and fennel
  salad, 81
  Classic coleslaw, 70
  Shaved fennel, melon and green olive
  salad, 88
  Slow-braised fennel, garlic, capers
  and lemon, 132
Fig, hazelnut and thyme pizza, 60
flatbreads
  Cucumber, hummus and flatbread, 62
  Italian flatbread, 206
  Pea and mint falafel flatbreads, 48–9
freekeh: Roast pumpkin, freekeh, lime
and coriander salad, 69
Fresh tomato pizza with kale pesto and
olives, 52
Fried tofu sandwich with Japanese
barbecue sauce, 56
fritters
  Banana fritters with cinnamon and
  nutmeg, 156
  Pea and mint falafel flatbreads, 49
  Potato rosti, 30
fruits *See under individual fruit*

G

ganache, 154, 172
garlic
  Baba ghanoush, 204
  Kale, garlic, shallots, capers and
  lemon, 138
  Kale, lemon, garlic and seed salad, 65
  Mashed potato with lemon and olive
  oil, 147
  nutritional value, 49
  Penne with roasted tomato, garlic and
  olives, 96

  Roast mushrooms with thyme and
  garlic breadcrumbs, 31
  Slow-braised fennel, garlic, capers
  and lemon, 132
  Spaghetti with mushrooms, thyme and
  garlic, 100
  Whole roast celeriac with thyme, garlic
  and black olive sauce, 116
ghrelin, 46
ginger: Pumpkin, ginger and coriander
soup, hemp seeds and cashew
cream, 38
grain, 8 *See also* freekeh
green beans: Braised green beans with
cherry tomatoes and paprika, 114
Green smoothie formula, 24
Grilled cos with chilli and almonds, 87
Grilled peaches, vanilla, maple and
nuts, 164

H

Harissa, 197
  Barbecued asparagus with harissa
  breadcrumbs, 126
Hasselback sweet potatoes, 134
hazelnut
  Nut butter, 210
  Rhubarb and coconut crumble, 158
hemp seeds
  Fresh tomato pizza with kale pesto
  and olives, 52
  nutritional value, 52
  Pumpkin, ginger and coriander soup,
  hemp seeds and cashew cream, 38
herbs, 6 *See also* basil; coriander; dill;
mint; parsley; tarragon; thyme
Homemade baked beans, 34
Homemade breadcrumbs, 205
horseradish
  nutritional value, 90
  Over-roasted beetroot with walnut and
  horseradish cream, 119
  Potato, horseradish and tarragon
  salad, 90

I

ice-creams: Banana and berry ice-
cream, 167
iron *See* non-haem iron
Italian flatbread, 206

K

kale
  Broccoli and kale soup, 41
  Fresh tomato pizza with kale pesto
  and olives, 52
  Green smoothie formula, 24
  Kale, garlic, shallots, capers and
  lemon, 138
  Kale, lemon, garlic and seed salad, 65
  Kale and cashew pesto, 202
  Minestrone, risoni and kale pesto, 42
  nutritional value, 41, 65
  Zucchini spaghetti, peas, asparagus
  and kale pesto, 102
kidney bean
  Black bean burger, sriracha,
  cucumber, coriander and cos, 108
  Spicy chilli beans, 94

L

leek
  Charred leeks with romesco, 145
  Mushroom and chestnut
  wellington, 123
  Parsnip and leek soup with black
  pepper breadcrumbs, 46
legume, 8
  nutritional value, 94
  See also black bean; cannellini bean;
  chickpea; kidney bean; lentil
lemon
  Kale, garlic, shallots, capers and
  lemon, 138
  Kale, lemon, garlic and seed salad, 65
  Mashed potato with lemon and
  olive oil, 147
  Slow-braised fennel, garlic, capers
  and lemon, 132
  Zucchini carpaccio with pine nuts,
  sultanas and lemon, 84
lentil
  Lentil, mushroom and asparagus
  salad, 76
  Lentil, spinach and sage soup, 44
  Lentil, sweet potato and mushroom
  shepherd's pie, 110–11
  Spicy chilli beans, 94
lettuce
  Black bean burger, sriracha,
  cucumber, coriander and cos, 108
  Grilled cos with chilli and almonds, 87
lime: Roast pumpkin, freekeh, lime and
coriander salad, 69

M

macadamia: Nut butter, 210
mango: Green smoothie formula, 24
maple syrup
Chocolate and salted caramel tart, 172
Chocolate ganache (Chocolate, date and walnut brownies), 154
Grilled peaches, vanilla, maple and nuts, 164
Rhubarb and coconut crumble, 158
Roasted pineapple with chilli, mint and maple, 180
Saffron and cardamom poached pears with cashew cream, 178
Sesame with maple carrots with baba ghanoush, 141
Slow-grilled cauliflower steaks with miso, soy, maple and sesame seeds, 120
Sweet pastry, 208
marinades
Chimichurri, 195
Harissa, 197
Mashed potato with lemon and olive oil, 147
melon *See* rockmelon
Minestrone, risoni and kale pesto, 42
mint
Braised zucchini with cherry tomatoes and mint, 131
Carrot, chickpea, cumin and mint salad, 74
Pea and mint falafel flatbreads, 48–9
Risi e bisi, 115
Roasted pineapple with chilli, mint and maple, 180
miso
Edamame hummus, 201
Slow-grilled cauliflower steaks with miso, soy, maple and sesame seeds, 120
Sticky eggplant with miso and sesame, 150
mousse: Chocolate mousse with berries and pistachios, 168
mushroom
Lentil, mushroom and aspargus salad, 76
Lentil, sweet potato and mushroom shepherd's pie, 110–11
Mushroom and chestnut wellington, 122–3
nutritional value, 76, 123
Roast mushrooms with thyme and garlic breadcrumbs, 31
Spaghetti with mushrooms, thyme and garlic, 100

N

no-bake desserts
Banoffee pie pots, 170
Chia, coconut and berry parfaits, 18
Chocolate chia seed puddings, 21
Chocolate, date and walnut brownie, 154
Chocolate mousse with berries and pistachios, 168
Summer pudding, 174
non-haem iron, 24
and cast iron pots, 34
food combinations to boost, 49, 94
Nut and seed mix, 213
Classic coleslaw, 70
Grilled peaches, vanilla, maple and nuts, 164
Kale, lemon, garlic and seed salad, 65
Roast pumpkin, freekeh, lime and coriander salad, 69
Nut butter, 210
nutmeg: Banana fritters with cinnamon and nutmeg, 156
nutritional yeast, 96
nuts, 8 *See also* almond; hazelnut; macadamia; pecan; pine nut; pistachio; walnut

O

oat
Apple and cinnamon breakfast cookies, 20
Banana, pecan, chia and strawberry pancakes, 23
Chocolate, cinnamon and apricot breakfast bars, 17
nutritional value, 17
Rhubarb and coconut crumble, 158
olive oil
nutritional value, 183
Pumpkin and olive oil spice cake, 182
olive
Black olive sauce, 190
Fresh tomato pizza with kale pesto and olives, 52
Penne with roasted tomato, garlic and olives, 96
Roast capsicum, capers, olives, chilli, 142
Shaved fennel, melon and green olive salad, 88
Whole roast celeriac with thyme, garlic and black olive sauce, 116
orange
Apple strudel, 160–1
Rhubarb and coconut crumble, 158
Shaved fennel, melon and green olive salad, 88
Orecchiette with cauliflower and peppery breadcrumbs, 99
Over-roasted beetroot with walnut and horseradish cream, 119

P

pancakes: Banana, pecan, chia and strawberry pancakes, 23
pantry staples, 6, 8
parsley
Braised green beans with cherry tomatoes and paprika, 114
Broccoli and kale soup, 41
Celeriac, radicchio and fennel salad, 81
Chimichurri, 195
Risi e bisi, 115
Roast capsicum, capers, olives, chilli, 142
Spaghetti with mushrooms, thyme and garlic, 100
Witlof, apple, radish and walnut salad, 82
Parsnip and leek soup with black pepper breadcrumbs, 46
pasta
Minestrone, risoni and kale pesto, 42
Orecchiette with cauliflower and peppery breadcrumbs, 99
Penne with roasted tomato, garlic and olives, 96
Spaghetti with mushrooms, thyme and garlic, 100
pastry
Apple strudel, 160–1
Chocolate and salted caramel tart, 172
Mushroom and chestnut wellington, 122–3
Sweet pastry, 208
Pea and mint falafel flatbreads, 48–9
peach
Green smoothie formula, 24
Grilled peaches, vanilla, maple and nuts, 164
pear
Saffron and cardamom poached

pears with cashew cream, 178
Shaved asparagus, pear, walnut and rocket salad, 66
pea
    Pea and mint falafel flatbreads, 48–9
    Risi e bisi, 115
    Zucchini spaghetti, peas, asparagus and kale pesto, 102
pecan
    Apple strudel, 160–1
    Banana, pecan, chia and strawberry pancakes, 23
    Banoffee pie pots, 170
    Nut butter, 210
Penne with roasted tomato, garlic and olives, 96
pepita: Nut and seed mix, 213
pesto: Kale and cashew pesto, 202
pie: Lentil, sweet potato and mushroom shepherd's pie, 110
pine nut
    Nut and seed mix, 213
    Zucchini carpaccio with pine nuts, sultanas and lemon, 84
pineapple
    Green smoothie formula, 24
    Roasted pineapple with chilli, mint and maple, 180
pistachio: Chocolate mousse with berries and pistachios, 168
pizzas
    Basic pizza dough, 207
    Fig, hazelnut and thyme pizza, 60
    Fresh tomato pizza with kale pesto and olives, 52
polyphenols, 24
poppyseed: Nut and seed mix, 213
potato
    Mashed potato with lemon and olive oil, 147
    Potato, horseradish and tarragon salad, 90
    Potato rosti, 30
    Shoestring chips with rosemary and sea salt, 149
prune: Chocolate, cinnamon and apricot breakfast bars, 17
puddings: Chocolate chia seed puddings, 21
pumpkin
    Pumpkin, ginger and coriander soup, hemp seeds and cashew cream, 38
    Pumpkin and olive oil spice cake, 182
    Pumpkin and sweet potato soup with sambal, 45
    Roast pumpkin, freekeh, lime and coriander salad, 69

Stuffed butternut pumpkin with sage, chestnuts and cranberries, 105
pumpkin seed See pepita

Q

quinoa: Stuffed butternut pumpkin with sage, chestnuts and cranberries, 105
quinoa flake: Chocolate, cinnamon and apricot breakfast bars, 17

R

radicchio: Celeriac, radicchio and fennel salad, 81
radish: Witlof, apple, radish and walnut salad, 82
raspberry: Chocolate mousse with berries and pistachios, 168
Rhubarb and coconut crumble, 158
rice
    Rice pudding and strawberry jam, 186
    Risi e bisi, 115
risoni: Minestrone, risoni and kale pesto, 42
Roast capsicum, capers, olives, chilli, 142
Roast mushrooms with thyme and garlic breadcrumbs, 31
Roast pumpkin, freekeh, lime and coriander salad, 69
Roasted pineapple with chilli, mint and maple, 180
rocket: Shaved asparagus, pear, walnut and rocket salad, 66
rockmelon: Shaved fennel, melon and green olive salad, 88
Romesco sauce, 192
    Charred leeks with romesco, 145
    Whole roast cauliflower, romesco and avocado, 106
rosemary: Shoestring chips with rosemary and sea salt, 149

S

Saffron and cardamom poached pears with cashew cream, 178
sage
    Lentil, spinach and sage soup, 44
    Stuffed butternut pumpkin with sage, chestnuts and cranberries, 105
salads
    Avocado, sprout and cucumber

salad, 73
    Carrot, chickpea, cumin and mint salad, 74
    Celeriac, radicchio and fennel salad, 81
    Classic coleslaw, 70
    Cucumber, sesame and chilli salad, 71
    Grilled cos with chilli and almonds, 87
    Kale, lemon, garlic and seed salad, 65
    Lentil, mushroom and asparagus salad, 76
    Potato, horseradish and tarragon salad, 90
    Roast pumpkin, freekeh, lime and coriander salad, 69
    Shaved asparagus, pear, walnut and rocket salad, 66
    Shaved fennel, melon and green olive salad, 88
    Tomato and beetroot salad, 78
    Witlof, apple, radish and walnut salad, 82
    Zucchini carpaccio with pine nuts, sultanas and lemon, 84
Sambal, 198
    Crispy brussels sprouts, parsley and sambal, 136
    Pumpkin and sweet potato soup with sambal, 45
sauces
    barbecue sauce (Fried tofu sandwich with Japanese barbecue sauce), 56
    Black olive sauce, 190
    Caramel sauce, 209
    Chimichurri, 195
    Harissa, 197
    Kale and cashew pesto, 202
    Romesco sauce, 192
    Sambal, 198
    Tomato basil sauce, 194
    See also marinades
Scrambled chickpeas, 26
sesame seed
    Cold spinach with toasted sesame seeds, 146
    Cucumber, sesame and chilli salad, 71
    Sesame with maple carrots with baba ghanoush, 141
    Slow-grilled cauliflower steaks with miso, soy, maple and sesame seeds, 120
    Sticky eggplant with miso and sesame, 150
shallot
    Kale, garlic, shallots, capers and

lemon, 138
Sambal, 198
Shaved asparagus, pear, walnut and rocket salad, 66
Shaved fennel, melon and green olive salad, 88
Shoestring chips with rosemary and sea salt, 149
silver beet: Green smoothie formula, 24
Slow grilled cauliflower steaks with miso, soy, maple and sesame seeds, 120
Slow-braised fennel, garlic, capers and lemon, 132
smoothie: Green smoothie formula, 24
soups
  Broccoli and kale soup, 41
  Lentil, spinach and sage soup, 44
  Minestrone, risoni and kale pesto, 42
  Parsnip and leek soup with black pepper breadcrumbs, 46
  Pumpkin, ginger and coriander soup, hemp seeds and cashew cream, 38
  Pumpkin and sweet potato soup with sambal, 45
soy milk
  Banana, pecan, chia and strawberry pancakes, 23
  Chia, coconut and berry parfaits, 18
  Fried tofu sandwich with Japanese barbecue sauce, 56
  Mashed potato with lemon and olive oil, 147
  Pumpkin and olive oil spice cake, 182
  Rice pudding and strawberry jam, 186
soybeans: Edamame hummus, 201
Spaghetti with mushrooms, thyme and garlic, 100
spices, 6
  Black bean burger, sriracha, cucumber, coriander and cos, 108
  Braised green beans with cherry tomatoes and paprika, 114
  Pumpkin and olive oil spice cake, 182
  Spicy chilli beans, 94
  See also cardamom; cinnamon, coriander; ginger; nutmeg
spinach
  Broccoli and kale soup, 41
  Cold spinach with toasted sesame seeds, 146
  Green smoothie formula, 24
  Lentil, mushroom and asparagus salad, 76
  Lentil, spinach and sage soup, 44
  Mushroom and chestnut wellington, 122–3
  nutritional value, 146

sprout: Avocado, sprout and cucumber salad, 73
Sticky eggplant with miso and sesame, 150
strawberry
  Banana, pecan, chia and strawberry pancakes, 23
  Chocolate mousse with berries and pistachios, 168
  Rice pudding and strawberry jam, 186
strudel: Apple strudel, 160–1
Stuffed butternut pumpkin with sage, chestnuts and cranberries, 105
sultana
  Carrot, chickpea, cumin and mint salad, 74
  Zucchini carpaccio with pine nuts, sultanas and lemon, 84
Summer pudding, 174
sunflower seed: Nut and seed mix, 213
Sweet pastry, 208
sweet potato
  Hasselback sweet potatoes, 134
  Lentil, sweet potato and mushroom shepherd's pie, 110–11
  nutritional value, 111
  Pumpkin and sweet potato soup with sambal, 45
  Sweet potato chips with chilli and dill, 59

T

tarragon: Potato, horseradish and tarragon salad, 90
tarts: Chocolate and salted caramel tart, 172
thyme
  Fig, hazelnut and thyme pizza, 60
  Roast mushrooms with thyme and garlic breadcrumbs, 31
  Spaghetti with mushrooms, thyme and garlic, 100
  Whole roast celeriac with thyme, garlic and black olive sauce, 116
tofu: Fried tofu sandwich with Japanese barbecue sauce, 56
tomato
  Braised eggplant, tomatoes, capers and basil, 130
  Braised green beans with cherry tomatoes and paprika, 114
  Braised zucchini with cherry tomatoes and mint, 131
  Eggplant parmigiana, 54
  Fresh tomato pizza with kale pesto

and olives, 52
  Homemade baked beans, 34
  Lentil, spinach and sage soup, 44
  Lentil, sweet potato and mushroom shepherd's pie, 110–11
  Minestrone, risoni and kale pesto, 42
  Penne with roasted tomato, garlic and olives, 96
  Romesco sauce, 192
  Spicy chilli beans, 94
  Tomato and beetroot salad, 78
  Tomato basil sauce, 194
tortillas: Breakfast burritos, 27
turmeric's nutritional value, 26

V

vitamin A, 111
vitamin B12, 96

W

walnut
  Banana, chia and walnut bread, 14
  Banoffee pie pots, 170
  Chocolate, date and walnut brownies, 154
  Nut butter, 210
  nutritional value, 66
  Over-roasted beetroot with walnut and horseradish cream, 119
  Rhubarb and coconut crumble, 158
  Shaved asparagus, pear, walnut and rocket salad, 66
  Witlof, apple, radish and walnut salad, 82
Whole roast cauliflower, romesco and avocado, 106
Whole roast celeriac with thyme, garlic and black olive sauce, 116
Witlof, apple, radish and walnut salad, 82
wraps: Breakfast burritos, 27

Z

zucchini
  Braised zucchini with cherry tomatoes and mint, 131
  Zucchini carpaccio with pine nuts, sultanas and lemon, 84
  Zucchini spaghetti, peas, asparagus and kale pesto, 102

LANTERN

UK | USA | Canada | Ireland | Australia
India | New Zealand | South Africa | China

Penguin Books is part of the Penguin Random House group of companies
whose addresses can be found at global.penguinrandomhouse.com.

Penguin
Random House
Australia

First published by Penguin Random House Australia Pty Ltd 2018

Text copyright © Tobie Puttock 2018
Photography copyright © Julie Renouf 2018

The moral right of the author has been asserted.

Cover and text design by Daniel New © Penguin Random House
Australia Pty Ltd
Cover and internal photography by Julie Renouf
Food styling by Lee Blaylock
Photography assistant: Jill Haapaniemi
Typeset in Helvetica LT Std by Post Pre-Press Group, Brisbane, Queensland
Colour separation by Splitting Image Colour Studio, Clayton, Victoria
Printed and bound in China by 1010 Printing International Ltd

NATIONAL
LIBRARY
OF AUSTRALIA

A catalogue record for this
book is available from the
National Library of Australia

ISBN: 978 0 14379 217 8

penguin.com.au

**The information contained in this book is of a general nature only.
If you wish to make use of any dietary information in this book relating
to your health, you should first consider its appropriateness to your
situation, including consulting a medical professional.**